5ᶜ

Scottish climbs: Volume 1

This pictorial guide is intended for those wishing to climb in
Scotland in summer or winter.

Volume 1 covers the areas of Arran, Arrochar, Glencoe,
Glen Etive, Garbh Bheinn and Ben Nevis.

Volume 2 covers the areas of Eigg, Skye (Cuillin, Blaven),
Harris, Creagh Meaghaidh, Binnein Shuas, Achnashellach,
Torridon (Coire Mhic Fhearchair, Carnmore, Applecross),
Stac Polly, Suilven, Fionaven, Old Man of Stoer,
Old Man of Hoy, Cairngorms.

Scottish climbs: Volume 1
Hamish MacInnes

A mountaineer's pictorial guide to climbing in Scotland

Constable London

First published in 1971 by
Constable & Company Ltd
10 Orange Street London WC2H 7EG

Second edition 1976

Copyright © Hamish MacInnes 1971

ISBN 0 09 457170 8
Printed in England at The Curwen Press Plaistow E13

The photographs were taken by the author
Maps and photographic art work by Graeme Hunter

To Ian, Jim and Tom
with thanks for
many happy
mountain days

Contents

Maps

Introduction

The routes described in this guide represent a cross section of
Scottish climbing. I am aware that many good climbs have
been omitted and some of doubtful quality included. This has
mainly been due to the photographic cover of the cliffs, but I
feel sure that in each area climbs are described which will suit
everyone. No one person has done all the routes described and
without the help of many colleagues it would have been
impossible for me to complete this work.

This guide book is intended as an introduction to some of the
Scottish climbing areas and is in no way a complete work.
Those who wish to climb in any particular area for any time
are strongly advised to purchase one of the Scottish Mountaineering Trust Guide Books, which cover in detail nearly all the
climbing grounds in Scotland. For an up-to-date account of
new routes the Scottish Mountaineering Club Journal
(published annually in May) should be purchased.

In view of the great scope of this book it is very difficult to
check these routes frequently, and I should appreciate hearing
of any inaccuracy or of changes of route due to rock fall etc.,
for alteration in future editions.

Hamish MacInnes
Glencoe, Argyll

Preface to Second Edition

There have been few changes in this second edition of *Scottish climbs*,
other than printing errors and the grades of certain winter routes.
I am indebted to climbers who have written in to me pointing
out these inaccuracies and I trust that any further errors will be
brought to my notice in the future.

Shortly after the publication of *Scottish climbs* there was a
revolution in ice climbing with the advent of the dropped pick. As
many climbers have not aspired to these new techniques, gradings
based on the use of traditional ice climbing equipment has been
retained.

For some time there has been a movement to resist the publication
of new routes in the North West Highlands. Though many new routes
have been done in areas described in Volume 2 of *Scottish climbs*, these
have not been included and it is to be hoped that this policy will
continue so that we may retain a climbing 'wilderness area' which will
lend itself to a certain quality of exploration for future generations.

Hamish MacInnes
September, 1975

Acknowledgements

Without the generous help of the undermentioned climbers this book would not have been possible.

D Alcock

J Ball

Mrs Ball

D Bathgate

D J Bennett

M Boyson

W D Brooker

P Buckley

A C Cain

I Clough

P Crew

J Cunningham

B Findlay

A Fyffe

J Grieve

J Hardie

J Hartley

J Hinde

D Lang

L S Lovat

J McArtney

M Main

J R Marshall

W H Murray

Dr T W Patey

J Porteous

N Quinn

M Rennie

R Richardson

D H Scott

R Sharp

W Skidmore

D Smith

W Smith

K Spence

W Sproul

D D Stewart

P Thomas

Dr W Wallace

P Walsh

K Wilson

Notes on the Use of the Guide

Route Grades, Rock
The International Union of Alpine Clubs system of rock climbing grading has been used throughout the text. This is as follows:

- I = Easy
- II = Moderate–Difficult
- III = Difficult–Very Difficult
- IV = Very Difficult–Severe
- V = Severe–Very Severe
- VI = Very Severe Upwards

Further subdivisions, + & —

Route Grades, Snow and Ice
The grading of winter routes has been described from Easy to Very Severe. A few routes as well as being Very Severe are serious undertakings and should only be attempted by climbers with considerable Scottish winter climbing experience. Some are technically very hard and/or difficult to retreat from or lacking in belays. These routes are marked Serious. If you have no previous experience of Scottish winter climbing, *only* attempt a route well within your capabilities. The times indicated with the routes gives only a rough guide for a competent party of two climbing.

Three Star Grading
A star system (* ** ***) has been adopted which gives a general indication of route quality. Three stars means that the route is a very fine one. The three star system is a quality guide to each particular area and indicates the relative merits of routes in each region.

Artificial Gradings
These are marked A1 and upwards.

Abbreviations
The abbreviations used throughout the text are obvious eg:
FA=First Ascent. FTR=First Traverse. ST=Stance. P=Piton. N, S, E, W=points of the compass. R=Right. L=Left. TR=Traverse. B=Belay.

Rope Lengths

Ropes of 120ft should be used, except on the harder routes, where 150ft may be necessary.

Scottish Winter Climbing

Over the past years a very high standard of ice climbing has evolved in Scotland. For someone not versed in this sport it is advisable to attempt the easier routes to begin with (some two standards below their normal summer rock climbing standard) rather than to get into difficulties.

Not only has the technical standard of the climb to be considered, but the condition of the snow and ice, the time factor and the weather. Bad weather can blow up very fast and a simple climb in fair weather can become a fight for survival in a blizzard. During mid-winter there is limited daylight and not only is it essential to set off at first light but one must learn to move fast and only have essential stops. Safe, fast climbing is probably the key to successful Scottish winter mountaineering.

Snow conditions

Snow is in a constant state of change and the process of firnification should be studied (see bibliography) by all who intend to winter climb. Generally speaking, firn snow and white ice give the best climbing conditions and green ice the best on steep ice pitches. On such steep ice, ice screws are now used extensively for belays and runners.

Often, after a heavy fall of snow, the lower gullies come into condition first and a number of these are described. Generally speaking, the big ice gullies seldom come into condition before late January and during February and March there is often adequate ice for climbing the steeper routes. There are many different types of snow and ice and the subject is too vast to deal with in a Guide Book. Make a point of studying these, first by reading the books mentioned, and then by observing when you are on the mountains.

Avalanches

Avalanches have become such a major aspect of Scottish winter accidents that some guidance is necessary to avoid further possible trouble. The simple rule of not climbing in gullies or on dangerous slopes, ie. steep, open slopes, especially convex ones, *during or immediately after a heavy snow fall*, should be strictly adhered to. Some 24 hours after a heavy fall, the snow has usually settled sufficiently to lessen the avalanche danger. The great majority of avalanche accidents occur during this danger period and if you feel that you must go out, keep to safe buttresses or ridges. Slopes of 14° and upwards can avalanche.

There are two common types of avalanches in Scotland, the wet snow and the slab avalanche. The wet snow avalanche usually starts in a gully or a slope with a harder underlayer which offers little adhesion to the fresh fall, or in the case of a heavy thaw, the water can run over this harder layer breaking what adhesion there is. The hard and soft slab avalanche are more difficult to predict, but again the 24 hour rule should be kept to. Avoid traversing potentially dangerous snow slopes.

A number of avalanches fall in the spring, usually of wet snow and the early start advocated elsewhere in the text, especially in sunny weather, should be the rule. Cornices can fall and these should be passed before any appreciable thaw has set in. Occasionally a gully whose cornice may have fallen can have a further dangerous cornice in a subsidiary hidden gully.

Judging snow conditions can take many years' experience, but the simple rules above and a working knowledge of snow structure can help a great deal in assessing a particular climb. Make a point of studying the books listed in the bibliography.

Basic Essentials for Winter Climbing
Check your equipment with this list before you embark on a climb.
1 Cleated rubber-soled boots.
2 Crampons.
3 Ice Axe.
4 One rope per party of two.
5 Windproof anorak/cagoule and trousers.
6 Woollen mitts and overmitts. Spare mitts.
7 Balaclava.
8 Relevant map in plastic bag.
9 Compass.
10 Torch or headlamp, with *new* battery and spare bulb.
11 Whistle.

12 Food and food for emergency use.
13 First Aid.
14 Helmet.
15 Bivouac sack.
16 Ice hammer, several pitons/dead man or ice screws,
   karabiners, slings and terrordactyls on all but the easiest routes.
17 Frameless rucksack.
18 Snow gaiters.
19 Spare pullover(s) or duvet, long Johns.

Do not forget to leave details of your proposed route.

When and where to climb

When and where to climb in Scotland is always a problem for
the English mountaineer and the chart of conditions (overleaf)
is only intended as a rough guide, for as everyone knows the
Scottish weather is fickle and conditions can change overnight.

Judging winter conditions can be especially difficult, and as
mentioned under the section on Avalanches it is better to keep
to ridges and buttresses if in doubt. This is especially true for
the climber with no Scottish winter experience as the winter
buttress routes are usually predictable and more akin to rock
climbing.

There are several months each year which are usually wet in
the Western Highlands and during the months October and
November the rock is usually wet on all the high mountains.
An ice-axe may well be needed from October until mid-May
in the West and through until July in the Cairngorms and on
Ben Nevis. The lower crags however are quite suitable for rock
climbing, though it can be cold.

As well as the weather and snow conditions there are other
factors which influence climbing in Scotland in certain seasons.
These are midges, stalking and grouse shooting. The midges are
usually plentiful from the end of June until the beginning of
September. In most areas deer stalking starts in early
September until the 20 October (but officially from the 20 July)
followed by hind shooting until the 15 February. With the
exception of certain areas marked, access is not always difficult
during the hind shooting. From the 12 August, grouse shooting
can affect low level access to certain areas. The best motto is
when in doubt ask locally.

The first week or so of May though often sunny can be wintry with possibly hard snow conditions and snow storms so one should not be caught unawares without winter clothing and climbing equipment.

When and where to climb

A rough guide to the Scottish climbing areas based on many years' climbing experience by leading Scottish climbers.

Key to Chart

** Applecross, Carnmore area and Stac Polly can provide rock climbing from March some years. Carnmore area is the most restricted area re stalking. see area introductions.

1 There is usually access if one keeps to the paths to Lochnagar and Creag an Dubh-Loch from Glen Muick.

Key to Symbols
d deer stalking
p powder snow
R primarily rock climbing
S winter climbing conditions
W often wet
M midges, possibly plentiful
m midges, not usually bad
r rock climbing on ridges, buttresses
s snow in gullies, possibly good
w often wet snow

Where S or s appears, snow climbing equipment should be taken. A question mark means doubtful.

Best months for climbing are in italic and apply mainly to leading symbol eg. *R*. possibly best for rock climbing.

NB Sunshine figures have not been included due to lack of accurate records in the mountainous areas.

	Dec	Jan	Feb	Mar	Apr	May	Jun	Jul	Aug	Sep	Oct
Arran	W	Sw	Sw	rS	R	R	R	Rm	Rmw	Rm	R?
Arrochar	W	S?	S?	RS	R	R	R	RmW	RmW	Rw	RW
Glencoe	S?	S	S	Sr	Rs	Rs	Rs	RmW	RmW	R	R?
Garbh Bheinn	S?w	S?w	S?	Rs	R?	R	R	RMW	RMW	Rwd	R?
Ben Nevis	S?	S	S	Sr	Sr	R	Rs	RsWm	RmW	R	
Skye	S?	S?	S?	Sr	Rs	Rs	Rs	RMW	RMW	R	R?
Harris	S?w	S?	S?	R?s	Rs	R	R	RMW	RMWd	Rd	R?
NW Scotland**	w	S?	S?	Rs	Rs	R	R	RMW	RMWd	Rd*	R?
Cairngorms N	Sp	S	S	S	Sr	Rs	Rs	Rsm	Rm	R	
Cairngorms S	Sp	S	S	Sr	Sr	Rs	Rs	Rm	Rm	Rd1	
Creagh Meaghaidh	S?	S	S	S	S?						
Etive Slabs				R?	R	R	R	RM	RM	Rm	R?

Accident Procedure

General
Keep calm. Take time to plan. Prevent further accident.
Reassure victim firmly and repeatedly if necessary. If un-
conscious ensure victim is breathing with clear airway, if not
Act at Once.

Unconscious Patient
1 Maintain an adequate airway, this is of over-riding impor-
tance. If the victim's chest is moving, but he is blue or making
choking noises, then the passage of air to lungs may be obstructed
by – *teeth, tongue, vomit,* or blood running from back of nose. *Snow*
from avalanche, etc. Open mouth, remove false teeth or teeth
knocked out in fall, pull tongue forward and hold chin up and
forward. Mop out (or suck out if tube available) any blood,
vomit or snow from back of throat and nose with rags, etc. If
airway is still obstructed turn patient gently onto abdomen,
head to one side and downhill. Kneel beside patient facing his
head, grasp chest by placing thumbs one on either side of spine
pointing towards his head, fingers round chest. Apply pressure
in rhythm with his breathing, and ensure air is passing freely.
This also helps to expel any fluids from airway.

Patient not Breathing
Clear airway as above, pinch victim's nose and breathe into his
mouth making sure chest rises. Do this at normal respiration
rate, until breathing re-starts. If this method is not effective
turn onto abdomen and proceed as above.

2 Stay with patient, keep him warm and secure. 3 *No Morphia*
or fluids. After regaining consciousness the victim can be allowed
to sit up, given a drink and may later walk down adequately
belayed and supported. Many are unconscious a relatively
short time, but remain confused and irresponsible, thus should
not be left. He may seem back to normal but may later become
confused again or even relapse into unconsciousness. If it is
imperative to leave an unconscious patient he must be adequately secured so that he can't sustain further injury or get lost
if he regains consciousness. Mark the place by cairn, etc., as
there may be no guiding call/signal for rescue parties and in
winter he could be quickly covered with snow.

Dead

The question of death can be very difficult in some cases. If there is any doubt, artificial respiration and/or external cardiac massage (by pressing firmly and regularly on the breast bone) should be carried out, until signs of death are clear or breathing starts again. Nearly all the commonly used signs of death, e.g., no pulse, apparently no breathing, muscular rigidity, pale 'dead-looking' patient can occur as a result of a drop in body temperature. Unless the victim has injuries clearly incompatible with life, it would be wiser to treat as alive until expert medical opinion is obtained. The 'apparently dead' person is in much greater need of urgent assistance than his injured companion – with say a broken leg. Remember the gravity of the decision when you decide someone is dead. When someone dies blood drains into whatever happens to be the lowest parts producing a bluish-red stain in the skin. It will not be present over areas subject to pressure, e.g., if lying on back, staining will be present at back of neck, and small of back, but not over shoulders and buttocks. This staining may be confused with bruising but with bruising there is usually localised swelling and possibly skin abrasions.

Morphia

May be given for severe pain and helps in shock and haemorrhage. Never give to someone who has been or is still unconscious – it may kill them. If morphia is given, the patient must be clearly labelled with time and dose.

Wounds

Cover with clean colour-fast cloth, pulling edges together by way in which dressings are applied.

Haemorrhage

Can be stopped by firm continued pressure by a small hand-held pad over the site of wound. Apply pressure for 15 mins. before relaxing. Don't remove pad but bandage firmly in position. Head wounds always bleed freely but bleeding can be stopped with a light bandage. Pressure should not be applied as this may drive fragments of bone into the brain.

Fractures and Sprains

Compare one limb with the other. If in doubt treat for fracture.

Splinting or immobilisation prevents further pain, shock and damage, and should be done as soon as possible. Always pad splints, a partially inflated jet splint can be used as padding. If jet splint is used alone take care to avoid over inflation.

Spine

Symptoms, pain in back and/or cannot feel or move legs or arms. Do not move until skilled help is available (only exception to this is in order to maintain clear airway). When stretcher arrives place a soft pad, e.g. pullover, to fill hollow of back on stretcher, if patient is lying on back on ground. If lying face down put on stretcher in this position. Move patient without in any way increasing or decreasing flexion of his spine, secure to stretcher in this position. Any movement of spine may result in permanent paralysis.

Limbs

Collar Bone and Upper Arm. Support weight of arm by scarf, etc. round wrist and neck. Place hand of injured arm near opposite shoulder and bandage forearm to chest. *Elbow*: do not attempt to bend or straighten arm. Splint as it lies, support weight of forearm. *Forearm and Wrist*. Improvise splint and strap lower arm to it. Support whole arm in sling, or bandage to body. *Thigh*: straighten good leg beside injured leg. If long straight splint is available place on outer side of injured leg from armpit to below foot and secure to body round chest. Place pads or padded splints between legs and tie both legs and this splint together at knees, ankles and upper thighs. Pass a bandage under injured thigh and up through crutch and tie (to include long splint) to chest bandage underneath armpits. Tie long splint to legs at upper thighs, knees, feet and ankles. *Lower Leg or Ankle*: slacken boot laces. Proceed as above but outer splint need only come to mid thighs. *Ribs*: no emergency treatment necessary.

Frostbite

Superficial: skin white and doughy – heat by applying body heat, e.g., hold affected part between hands, etc. Protect from further cold. Do not rub, or rub with snow. *Deep*: white and hard – do not give any first aid treatment; keep parts cool.

Exposure

Symptoms: any of the following – Disturbances of speech and/
or vision, irrational behaviour, lethargy, shivering, stumbling.
Treatment – Act at once. Do not allow serious disability or
collapse to develop. Prevent further heat and energy loss, e.g.,
rest, shelter from wind, bivouac sack, windproof clothing to
include head and neck. Give glucose, sweet warm drinks, etc.
No alcohol. Reassure patient, as fear greatly accelerates
exhaustion.

General

Send a competent member of party for help by safe route *after*
injuries have been assessed, and it is known what type of help is
needed. Messenger should leave spare clothing, etc. and mark
position of patient on map before leaving. He should look back
whilst descending to note landmarks. In bad weather move
injured person carefully to level sheltered place provided there
are no spinal injuries and after other injuries have been dealt
with. Place rucksack, ropes, heather or something waterproof
underneath, and as many layers as possible on top, massaging
uninjured limbs, hands, etc. will help to keep circulation going.
If victim cannot be moved, keep him warm and sheltered
(build snow/rock wall or lie to windward). Slacken boots, but
leave on if foot or ankle injured, otherwise remove. Wrap up
feet and place in rucksack to prevent frostbite. Do not give
alcohol, but other fluids may be given provided no internal
injuries suspected. In latter case allow mouthfuls of fluid or
chips of ice to moisten mouth and then be spat out. Whilst
awaiting stretcher continue to give distress signals to attract
any nearby climbers. *International Alpine Distress Signal* – Light,
Sound, etc., six flashes/notes at ten second intervals followed by
sixty second pause. SOS · · · – – – · · · can also be used. Red
Flare is also used for distress. *For help dial 999 ask for Police.*

Sense on the Scottish Hills

'Look well to each step'

Climb if you will, but remember that courage and strength are nought without prudence, and that a momentary negligence may destroy the happiness of a lifetime. Do nothing in haste; look well to each step; and from the beginning think what may be the end. Edward Whymper

1. Seek advice daily about local conditions and problems. Beware of avalanches and dangerous corniced ridges. Pay attention to weather forecasts. If bad stay in the valleys; conditions on Scottish tops can become Arctic.
2. Never go alone, but keep parties small, with an experienced leader. Don't separate. Leave a note of route planned and report forced changes at earliest opportunity.
3. Plan your expedition with a safety margin and turn back while there is yet time. Before starting note local rescue posts.
4. Wear tricouni nailed boots in winter or crampons: vibrams are dangerous on hard snow and ice.
5. Carry an ice-axe and practise braking. Also reserve food, torch, whistle and watch.
6. Wear warm and windproof clothes. Carry extra for tops, halts and cold.
7. Take a 1 inch map and know how to use it with a suitable compass (e.g. prismatic or 'Silva').
8. If lost or caught in a blizzard, keep calm; seek or build temporary shelter. Vital energy can be lost fighting the wind – a dangerous foe.
9. If there is an accident send written message to nearest rescue post, giving accident position accurately. One member should stay with victim.
10. Learn life-saving first aid and carry simple first aid kit.
    Copies of Mountain Rescue & Cave Rescue can be obtained from Mountain Rescue Committee, Hill House, Cheadle Hulme, Stockport, Cheshire.
    Issued by the Mountain Rescue Committee of Scotland.

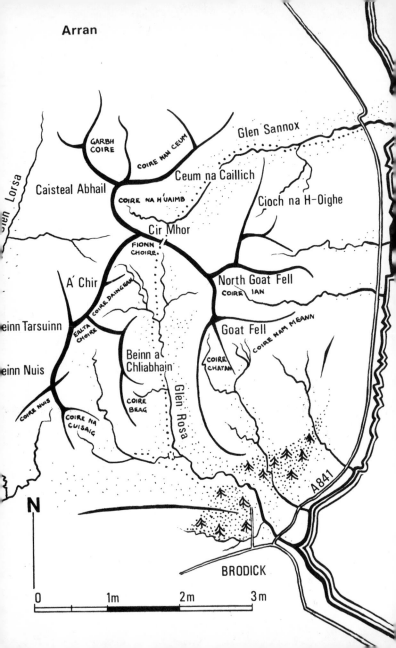

Isle of Arran, General

Arran lies in the Firth of Clyde and like all Scottish 'hill' islands it has its own peculiar charm. Not only have its mountains a certain gentle attraction, but the weather is often better than that of mainland mountains and indeed frequently when it is wet to the north Arran basks in sunshine.

Goat Fell is the highest peak on the Island – 2866ft. The peaks are the remains of a dome of very coarse-crystalled granite which provides ample friction for climbing except when wet, when lichen makes sections rather slippery. Cracks are not too frequent for piton belays.

Access

There are British Railways steamers operating all the year round from Ardrossan and Fairlie. Sunday sailings, June–September. It can be expensive to take a car to Arran, and if you intend to stay only a few days it is not worth while. Bicycles can be hired and in any case it is only a few miles' walk from Brodick Pier to Glen Rosa, or a bus service goes past Glen Sannox (infrequent).

Camping/Accommodation

Both Glen Rosa and Glen Sannox offer superb camp sites beside clear pools with unrestricted views of Cir Mhor, which, like the Matterhorn, is shapely on all sides. For doing a selection of the climbs mentioned in this guide probably Glen Rosa offers the best base. There are numerous boarding houses on the Island and a few hotels and details of these can be obtained from the local tourist office in Brodick or from the Scottish Tourist Board.

Map: os 1 inch 66.

Guide Books: Arran. Glen Rosa and Glen Sannox Basins. W W Wallace. SCOTTISH MOUNTAINEERING TRUST.

Mountain Rescue

Local Rescue Team. Official MR Post, Police Station, Brodick. Telephone Brodick 100 or 999.

Provisions
Supplies can be obtained at either Brodick or Corrie, early closing day Wednesday.

Traverse of A'Chir Ridge
Grade II: FTR *J H Gibson & two others 1892*
This is a fine narrow ridge and its traverse can be combined with a climb on Cir Mhor if approaching from Glen Rosa. A good route is up Cnoc Breac from Glen Rosa, along the ridge to Beinn a'Chliabhain, descend to col and take R path below rock face to gain ridge. The actual summit of A'Chir 2335ft is a massive boulder with at least three routes up it. The descent to the *mauvais pas* is on the w side and is well nail-marked. The *mauvais pas* occurs where the ridge levels, after the steep step. Just beyond, on the R descend a 14ft wall leading to a grass ledge slanting down out of sight. This becomes a rock trench near its end and leads to a small col at the base of an overhang. The following section gives pleasant climbing.

1.2 Old East
200ft grade II: FA *G H Townend, J Jenkins 1946*
Access route from Sub Rosa Gully to Terrace (and vice versa). Start close as possible to precipitous wall of Upper Pinnacle. Up direct 15ft slant L beneath overhang. Keep close to base of cliff, ascend steep slab to L of small chimney and up to Terrace.

1.3 Rosa Pinnacle East Face, Minotaur
175ft grade v+*: FA *D McKelvie, D Sim 1958*
On SE edge of Upper Pinnacle an obvious crack goes up and ends near Eyrie. Its line is parallel to top edge of South Ridge. From Sub Rosa Gully, easy up to small grass ledge below R angled corner to start of crack. Up crack (hard) to heather patch below start of overhang. P in L wall; 30ft. Next overhanging section is strenuous then 10ft up it's possible to get into crack (slim people, runner). Jam (face L), up chimney until exit on to rib, L, leading to broader upper chimney; 35ft. Up chimney, direct (this widens to a gully) and leave on R of large boulder; 110ft. Beyond pitch 4, grass ledge of Labyrinth is gained over rock-rib on R.

1 Cir Mhor, South East Face. 1 Start of South Ridge Direct

3

1.4 **Bluff**

250ft grade VI** : FA *H Donohoe, E McLellan 1968*

Follows true s face of Upper Rosa Pinnacle. Some way up Old
East the s face is patchworked with cracks. Cairn. Climb crack
(strenuous and delicate), to gain edge leading to spike in
corner. Up corner to grassy platform, P B; 35ft. Follow corner
above to next grass ledge, P B; 20ft. Using jammed sling move
into shallow chimney, climb to bulge. Move R below overlap
to downward sloping ledge which follows to ST and B; 35ft.
Up scoop above to runner in corner and move R on slabs (holds
above overlap). Continue round corner, insert P, tension to
crack on slab edge. Up crack and TR R into large corner, small
ST and P B; 90ft. L from B and up groove above; 70ft. Usual
route to summit of pinnacle.

1.5 **Prospero's Peril**

440ft grade V** : FA *G H Townend, G C Curtis 1943*

One must reach a horizontal ledge on crest above small vertical
undercut wall. Start below wall and TR obliquely R to scoop,
or climb scoop from bottom. Scoop leads to the ledge on crest.
A short groove then goes up to concave slab. TR up to L edge
of slab, then straight up to big grass platform by open corner
(crux). Or, TR R from concave slab into upper part of chimney-
crack which leads to platform. Note: the base of this chimney
lies a few feet to R of initial scoop and is an alternative start;
6oft. Go round corner on R, ascend undercut chimney; 40ft.
Easy to big ledge; 8oft. Up scoop on L until possible to TR R
to base of a curving flake-crack. Up to crest. Go on R wall (a
few feet), then up to small niche. Take inclined ledge to B
under overhanging block; 70ft. Climb slab-wall on L by crack,
then up slab to B under R – angled corner; 40ft. Reach big
slab by R – angled corner; 10ft and take grassy groove. A grass
patch leads to wall-edge of last slab (split by small chimney);
B; 100ft. Overhanging chockstone, and up into cleft, easy to
top; 50ft.

2.1 **Caliban's Creep**

500ft grade III +** : FA *G Curtis, G Townend 1943*

Gain highest of overlapping slabs from R, go round under L

corner of vertical wall to B (boulders on W side); 100ft. Out to
broken steep corner and an upward TR (exposed) round to
base of chimney on steep face, B; 50ft. Up chimney to B on
wide inclined roof; 50ft. Easy over slabs to top of level ridge,
that ends against vertical wall. Exit through rock tunnel R to B
(the Creep); 75ft. Along rock ledge round to steep E face and
enter deep cut chimney; 30ft. Ascend chimney (turns into big
trench) to ST below lip; 35ft. Easy climbing to top; 170ft.

2.2 Rosa Pinnacle, Fourth Wall

400ft grade IV**: FA *G Townend, H Moneypenny 1945*
Up grassy groove to turf ledge; 60ft. Up groove continuation;
60ft. Straight up rib on L (SW Slabs route goes R); 40ft. Fault
now grassy 40ft (keep L to big platform); 45ft. Cracks and
grooves to top of big rock plinth against face; 120ft. Up
chimney above plinth (a few ft) and by small ledge on R quit
chimney and onto wall. Up 6ft then downward TR until slab
can be ascended. An awkward R move leads into easy groove;
60ft. Gain terrace up rocks (easy); 20ft.

2.3 Sou'wester Slabs

340ft grade III +***: FA *G Townend, G Curtis, H Hore,
M Hawkins 1944*
Pitches 1, 2 & 3. As for Fourth Wall. A downward TR R leads to
open chimney-crack. Ascend to B; 50ft. Up twin flake cracks
to square cut lip of big slab, then down and on to sloping ST
(thread B); 55ft. Go R up further slab below big overhang to
B in level scoop; 50ft. TR below overhang and round corner to
big ledge on South Ridge below Three Tier Chimney of South
Ridge Direct; 30ft. Upper part of this route is followed.

2.4 West Flank Route

460ft grade −VI**: FA *W Skidmore, R Richardson, J Madden,
J Crawford 1963*
Starts at tapering two tier chimney below Sou'wester Slabs.
Up lower part of chimney to block B, ST. Strenuous; 60ft.
Ascend narrowing second chimney (strenuous) to ST and B;
50ft. Follow shallow score in great slab above direct to over-
hang at top, TR R to niche, P B; 90ft. L round corner into groove,
follow over bulge and layback up rounded corner to spike.
Above spike go L out of groove and up to P runner in horizontal
crack. Descend L down slab to break in overlap, climb to

thread B of Sou'wester Slabs; 100ft. Up corner above, step L to platform with block; 30ft. Up edge of slab to big overhang. Semi-hand TR L to good holds and on to small ST & P B; 50ft. Up broken slab to block B; 40ft. Climb diagonal fault to fault to terrace; 40ft.

2.5 Anvil
180ft grade —VI*: FA *D McKelvie, R Richardson 1960*
Start at broad crack (cairn) 100ft down from Sou'wester Slabs. Up crack to ST just L of small overhang; 25ft. Descend 10ft and TR R (delicate) to reach holds leading up through overhang to sloping platform, then by thin obvious crack to grass ledges and B on R; 70ft. Follow up L by grooves to cave & B; 60ft. Awkwardly out by R wall to gain easy slab leading to crest of South Ridge (top of pitch 4 of that route).

2.5a Anvil, Recess Start
130ft grade —VI**: FA *W Skidmore, J Madden, J Crawford 1964*
Some 40ft downhill from Anvil a gritty ledge goes horizontally across front of s ridge above lower slabs. A short distance along ledge an open groove runs up L. Climb groove to its end at B; 50ft. Round L, gain slab above and up direct then R to bottom of flake lodged beneath R wall of huge inverted V-shaped recess. Climb flake to spike runner, step L to opposite wall and pull up (high holds) to gain slab above (sustained pitch). Up groove on R, at top move L to low thread B of Anvil; 80ft. Finish via Anvil.

2.5b Anvil, Variation Finish
80ft grade V*: FA *R Richardson, J Madden 1965*
From cave B at top of Anvil's second pitch, TR L below overlap to groove and corner. Up corner (P runner) and bulge at top leading to easy slab to R of layback crack pitch of s ridge direct.

2.6 South Ridge Direct
855ft grade —VI***: FA *J Hamilton, D Paterson 1941*
Climb starts at obvious rock crevasse 60ft under and to R of the S-shaped crack, on a level with jammed boulders in Sub Rosa Gully. This can be reached by rising TR across slabs from L, 200ft (or more directly by steep groove close to Sub Rosa Gully). Go up above crevasse and take L slanting groove to level ledge below s crack, B; 60ft. Up crack to ledge (triangular

block B); 40ft. Up over overhanging wall by Y-shaped cracks (hard); 26ft. On up slabs to stony terrace; 20ft. TR L across top of big slab to B in far corner; 130ft. Up flake by crack (layback) to delicate R TR across base of higher slab until possible to go up to broad platform; 60ft. Or avoid TR by a continuous layback, R by undercut edge to L of higher slab. (Lovat's variation strenuous.) Pitches 5 and 6 can be missed by going directly up deep cut chimney above terrace on R or by TR further round to R and reaching ledge by open groove and wall (on E). (Though harder these variations are good.) Up into tri-partite chimney above ledge, to gain B on crest of ridge, over 2 slabs divided by short wall; 90ft. Up on edge of obvious arete; 60ft. Up to sloping Terrace (walk) under Upper Pinnacle. Reach roof of first slab stepping off flake just L of corner (knob-like holds). Directly up to fault on L. Up this to chimney (B); 90ft. Ascend chimney; 40ft. Reach level grass ledge. Go along until possible to ascend on to slab on R. Up to edge. ST at corner above poor B; 120ft. At holdless part of ridge TR on to E face to R angled corner under summit on outward sloping shelf. Up corner crack then short slab to summit.

2. R **Rosetta Stone**

Grade V+ : FA *R Smith 1957*
This is on W side of Pinnacle past top of Pinnacle Gully. A rope can be passed over the top for protection, or climb free.

3. 2 **Labyrinth**

400ft grade IV** : FA *G Curtis, H Moneypenny 1943*
Enter Labyrinth by an alley below R end of wall above Sub Rosa Gully. Easy inclined floor of alley or chimney and up and out through hole on L. Follow up to grassy ledge against wall; 70ft. Ascend corner and next chimney to ST, B; 30ft. On up chimney to angled grass step. Go across wall on L into small corner, under overhang. P B; 50ft (crux). Straight up (straddle) to tilted grass ledge. Round wall on R into deep chimney, B; 40ft. Straight up and come out on grass ledge; 30ft.

---

3 Arran, Rosa Pinnacle, East Face, Cir Mhor. 1 Minotaur (hidden). 5 Prow. PG Pinnacle Gully

Go behind chockstones above to rock ledge (the Eyrie); 35ft.
(There are 2 groups of chockstones, go over 1st and behind
2nd.) From Eyrie move R under the Prow into base of long
crack. Continue TR R via narrow ledge to easier ground and
access to wide grassy rake; 40ft. Take rake and small chimney
to big blocks; 85ft. Descend past blocks and go into and up
steep chimney above Pinnacle Gully. A slab then leads to top;
35ft.

3.2a Stewart Orr's Variation

135ft grade V: FA *J Stewart Orr, J MacLaurin 1951*
From Eyrie go directly up (easy rock) to big corner; 38ft.
There is a weird flange, on E wall. Layback on this and jam R
foot in corner crack, then reach ledge above. TR L on ledge and
round bulge. A short slab goes to S Ridge, just before TR on
last pitch of S Ridge.

3.3 Easter Route

335ft grade V+**: FA *K Barber, S Piggott 1938*
Start halfway between R corner of wall and Labyrinth. Easy
to big leaning block at base of chimney-crack; 65ft. Up crack
to grass ledge with boulders; 70ft. On up chimney to further
grass patch; 30ft. Labyrinth can be joined on L, on R a ledge
(with a big block) goes into Pinnacle Gully. Up vertical
chimney, then out R to tiered ledge (big turf sloping cap); 40ft.
TR horizontal cracks L to edge. Up direct to grass ledge; 40ft.
TR L to B at base of obvious crack, curving up R of the Prow (the
Eyrie is just L); 28ft. Climb curving crack (facing R); 40ft
(crux). On up crack to exit on summit ledge.

3.3a Double Crack Variation

Grade IV+**: FA *W Wallace, J Johnstone 1958*
The Pinnacle Gully wall of Rosa Pinnacle has an obvious
R-angled corner, 30ft high. The walls are IV by vertical cracks.

4 *Opposite:* The crux pitch on South Ridge Direct, Cir Mhor, Arran

5 *Overleaf left:* Looking across from the easier upper section of
South Ridge of Cir Mhor to Goat Fell. Glen Rosa is to right

7 *Overleaf right:* Sou'wester Slabs, Cir Mhor, Arran. Fourth Wall
climb is below, going up right

Using jams reach the Turf Cap at top of pitch 4, Easter Route. This Route is followed. This variation shortens climb (by 150ft).

9.1 April Arete
400ft grade −v* : FA *J Simpson, W Wallace 1959*
Follows L edge of gully A, exposed in places (some loose rock). One P B used, several good ST and B.

9.2 B2-C Rib
240ft grade III+* : FA *Messrs J Bell, Boyd, Green, Napier 1895*
NE Face, Cir Mhor (approach via Glen Sannox or from Glen Rosa/Sannox Saddle).
The rib consists of a number of slabs and ledges. Take line of least resistance. At final overhang, move out from niche (B on L) then straight up.

9.3 Pothole Slab
380ft grade −VI** : FA *W Skidmore, J Gillespie 1968*
Start at cairn at centre of slab. A few feet up to R is curious water-filled hole. Straight up slab to grass clump, ledge, P B; 90ft. Follow micro granite vein R to another clump, continue TR until possible to go straight up to big grass ledges, P B; 100ft. Up more broken ground just R of two pale rock scars to recess, P B under final cracks; 100ft. Exit on R, up bulge, move L to flake crack now visible. Use P runner, and climb crack (strenuous) to groove leading out to top; 90ft.

9.4 Bell's Groove
200ft grade III* : FA *J H Bell, Green 1894*
Go down 100ft from top of Eastern Stoneshoot then up into niche (grassy) on L. Up short chimney at rear and up back of

6 *Previous page left:* Looking across to Sou'wester Slabs, Cir Mhor, Arran. The route follows the crack system and goes up to the roof up right from climber

8 *Previous page right:* The upper traverse on West Flank Route. The route goes up the edge of the slab in the foreground, then across left

9 *Opposite:* Cir Mhor, North East Face. Glen Rosa/Sannox Saddle to left of Route 1

Goat Fell

To a'chir →

ES.

4

3

2

1

big block. Up to horizontal platform (at back a chimney-crack trends up L, The Groove). Straightforward above (usually greasy).

10.1 Coire Daingean Face, Boundary Ridge

38oft grade III* : FA *G Curtis, G Townend (alternate leads)* ;
H Moneypenny, H Dunster (alternate leads) 1943
Route follows L edge of face. Reach crest notch by scrambling, 6oft from bottom. Up slab to block on crest. Up, or round (L) into grassy gully to B; 7oft. Climb narrow crack to big spike abutting wall on R; 65ft. Up wall above spike and up further crack to base of steep edge on R; 7oft. Climb edge to ledge, TR short way R then up steep slab and easy ground to blocks on ledge over Boundary Gully; 6oft. (Ledge can also be gained by chimney (III), entered by TR L towards Boundary Gully.) Up on to long level ledge going across face, follow; 3oft. Up over slab above, trend up L to wall with small Y-shaped crack. Up crack to wide rock shelf, 112ft wall to top.
Variation 1 : Up open corner at back of blocks (top of pitch 4). Move on to shelf on R. Y-shaped crack is a few feet above (−v).
Variation 2 : From ledge under open corner of Variation 1 a ledge goes across vertical face above Boundary Gully. It steepens quickly and ends in a flake (overhanging). Follow ledge, up flake, move up R wall onto terrace to join original route. This is best variation (−v).

10.2 Pagoda Ridge

7ooft grade IV*+ : FA *G Townend, G Curtis 1943*
The route goes up R edge of Gully 4, but starts at lowest slabs on R. Up grassy crack that ends in sharp flake. L TR up to heather then L across slab to ST below overhang; 9oft. Up onto sloping shelf, follow to edge. 3oft higher is a side B; 9oft. Up edge R to blocks on edge of big heather patch; 6oft. Ascend wall above by short crack. A few feet further to ST at rear of block overhanging Gully; 6oft. Across slab above to small niche (spikes of rock on R); 3oft (crux). Move round corner on R, then TR concave slab to short wall above. Climb it L to R. Then L to edge, B; 8oft. Ascend crack above, B and up edge that steepens to a vertical wall. Climb wall (grooves and blocks)

10 Arran : A'Chir, East Face. Access from Glen Rosa by Coire Daingean or via the A'Chir Ridge approach mentioned in text

and B between two boulders; 112ft. Continue up crest of ridge; 180ft.

10.3 Slab and Flake Route

360ft grade IV+ : FA *G Townend, G Curtis, H Dunster 1943*
On bottom part of buttress is steep rock. Upper section has many grass ledges. Start at bottom L corner of big slab forming base of buttress and ascend close to L edge to ST; 30ft. Up (projecting hold above), then R up slab until possible to slant L to edge by big triangular flake (thread B); 60ft. Up L edge of flake, cross ledge to B. On up by R edge of flake, strenuous; 35ft. Up cleft trending R at rear of large flake (chockstone); 20ft. At top L edge of flake go across on opposite steep wall (crux) to heather ledge, or climb wall from top part of flake by undercut crack. Along heather ledge R past narrow crack to base of series of pigeonhole holds to B on ledge above; 38ft. Ascend ramp on R to shelf going L to further shelf. Go R up slab to B; 90ft. Up corner above B to open stony terrace. Cross this to B on wall behind (below broken rock spur); 25ft. Ascend spur and slab above. TR R to block B; 38ft. Up wall and wide crack to grass terrace and top of buttress; 45ft.

11.1 Brachistochrone

900ft grade VI+** : FA *M Galbraith, A McKeith 1966*
On S side of face are two parallel cracks leading directly to summit of buttress. Route follows L crack. Scramble up first 100ft of crack. Continue in crack, first by a chimney (IV+, wet) then over a flake overhang (VI, strenuous) and up twin cracks (−V, wet) to B on sloping ledge under huge roof; 150ft. Climb twin overhanging cracks above through roof (VI+, strenuous, 1 wedge, 3P, wet) to a block B in chimney; 50ft. TR ledge on L and layback up R to grass ledge above chimney (V) follow crack above over smooth bulge (V+, wet) to next roof. Climb an overhanging crack into sloping recess in roof (VI+, very wet) then swing down L (1 P wet) on to steep slab and go straight up to grass ledge and block B; 150ft. Continue 300ft by grassy cracks, slabs, corners and flakes (III), across Meadow Slabs to reach the continuation of the L crack in upper slabs. Finish up crack over three overlaps, detouring to R at second (−V).

11 Beinn Tarsuinn (Meadow Face), T marks the Terrace. Consolation Tor is to the right, out of picture

Note: An escape can be made at 2/3 height from both Bogle and Brachistochrone down easy terrace.

11.2 Bogle

820ft grade VI** : FA *I G Rowe, I Dundas 1967*

The route follows R of two great parallel cracks splitting face. The L-hand crack is Brachistochrone. Cracks split the big overhang at 250ft. R-hand crack continues above overhang as the cave pitch of the Rake and continues on the Meadow Slabs where crack divides, splitting the large square summit block. Scramble up 50ft, B and continue in line of crack with few and minor variations for two pitches until a slab is reached below large overhang (190ft V and V+). Here the crack bulges and passes overhang on R. Move up onto pedestal at 6ft and climb crack for 20ft (3 P runners, VI, strenuous, slimy, etrier used on last P). Move 10ft R (P) and climb parallel crack (15ft, 3 P, A2). B on ledge above. Continue in crack (80ft V) and climb slimy cave above by contortionate through route (40ft V+) (common to the Rake). Move L up inclined slab and B above it (20ft V+). Scramble up below Meadow Slabs; 200ft. Climb continuation of crack up to large summit block (160ft, IV, V). Here crack divides, climb two L-hand cracks (80ft, V+, V).

11.3 The Rake

480ft grade V+** : FA *W Skidmore, R Richardson 1962*

This route is on the overlapping slabs L of Meadow Grooves and, in middle part, uses hidden grass rake running up L. Starts few feet L of Meadow Grooves and R of big slab at broken rocks. Straight up rocks by rib; B (Letter R marked on rock); 40ft. Straight up by corners and grooves, then cross to grass rake on R to obvious block B; 65ft. Follow rake up L to finish below slab and unpleasant corner; P B on R wall; 150ft. Climb slab, passing spike runner on R wall, TR L below bulges, up to grass ledge; P B; 40ft. Up then round R into corner (good runner); with P for direct aid climb corner above and gain obvious bay on R; follow crack in slab on L and rock ledges to grass ledges and B; 100ft (crux). Climb corner to grass ledge and P B in overhanging cave; 35ft. Cave pitch on Bogle common to the Rake. Go up back of cave, stomach-traverse along ledge on L and gain slab and groove on other side of roof, following them to choice of B; 50ft. 50ft of scrambling lead to Terrace.

11.4 **Meadow Grooves**

320ft grade IV*: FA *G Curtis, H Moneypenny, E Morrison 1944*
Follow grooves up easier angled section of face to R of overlapping slabs. Follow heather gangway, start in groove furthest
L. A large slab and short groove go up in direction of two overlapping steps. TR to R, below steps, B below 15ft wall; 80ft.
Climb wall L to R (crux). Step into water-worn scoop; 90ft
(straightforward). Up to small amphitheatre; 50ft. Climb
chimney on R until forced to R and up two narrow chimneys;
80ft. Continue to platform leading to terrace; 90ft.

Arrochar (The Cobbler), General

The Cobbler, which is just a short way off the main Loch
Lomond road (A82) at Tarbet is a much neglected mountain by
the Sassenach. The mountain rises to the north-west of Loch
Long and the well known road, the Rest and Be Thankful
skirts its southern slopes.

The peak, which is seen to advantage from Tarbet on a clear
day, consists of three separate peaks: The North, the Cobbler's
Last, the Centre Peak, which is the summit and the South
Peak, known as the Cobbler's Wife – Jean. The mountain is
also known as Ben Arthur.

The rock is a silvery mica-schist providing holds which are
often embedded quartz, which requires a bit of getting used to
and can afford fine balance climbing on some of the steeper
walls. It can be very greasy in the wet.

Access

There is a daily bus service from Glasgow to Arrochar and
there is plenty of space for parking on the A83 near torpedo-
testing station on Loch Long. From here follow the left side of
the Allt a'Bhalachain (Buttermilk Burn) to the lower reaches
of the Cobbler, passing on the way the Shelter Stone and
Narnain Boulder – both offer sport in the form of rock problems.

Camping/Accommodation

There is an official camping site at Ardgartan as well as a
Youth Hostel and unrestricted camping in the Eastern Corrie
of the Cobbler. There are also a number of hotels in Arrochar
as well as boarding houses and for more frugal accommodation
there are many howffs (shelter stones) of various degrees of
comfort. These are mostly located in the high corrie to the
east and below the col separating the Centre and North Peak
of the Cobbler, and the Shelter Stone mentioned above.

Map : os Tourist Map Loch Lomond and the Trossachs.

Guide Book : Arrochar. J Houston, B H Humble SCOTTISH
MOUNTAINEERING TRUST.

Mountain Rescue
Local Police Rescue Team. Official MR Post, Mr J Paterson, Succoth Farm, Arrochar. Telephone Arrochar 241 or 999.

Provisions
Food can be bought at Arrochar, no early closing day.

13.1 Porcupine Wall

145ft grade V AI*: FA *H MacInnes, J Cunningham 1951*
Start some distance down W face under conspicuous corner with overhanging R wall (start hidden on illustration). TR along grass ledge L to R, climb direct up thin crack in overhanging R wall (some P). Pitch finishes on grass ledge L; 40ft. Step across top of Pitch 1 and TR round corner R, then slant up to rock shelves on L; 30ft. Move L to short wall, climbed from L to R, follow grass ledges to overhung corner. Climb corner direct to large ledge; 55ft.

13.2 Ithuriel's Wall

245ft grade —VI**: FA *H MacInnes 1952*
Start at cairn 100ft up and L of basin below Ardgartan Arete. Climb a broken fault diagonally R to terrace; 80ft. Climb corner above a flake B to ledge with large block on L; 25ft. Climb corner above; 8ft (with aid of P, move round to ledge on R). TR R and climb crack to higher ledge (P in Gladiator's Groove as B); 40ft. Move L and make awkward move into groove which is climbed to ledge and flake B (P used); 30ft. TR L 50ft and climb obvious fault to grass ledge with large block; 70ft.

13.3 Gladiator's Groove

210ft grade —VI***: FA *W Smith, H MacInnes 1951*
Start as for Ithuriel's Wall. Climb broken fault to terrace and TR R along terrace to P B at top of Pitch 2, Ardgartan Arete; 110ft. TR 10ft L, follow steep groove to small ledge, then move L to recessed corner (P runner). Climb awkward corner to upper ledge (flake B); 60ft. Climb bulging crack on R to sloping shelf and follow an upper crack to finish on slab, B; 40ft.

12 The Cobbler from the Shelter Stone. SP=South Peak. CP=Centre Peak. NP=North Peak

13.4 **Gladiator's Groove** Direct Start

140ft grade —VI***: FA *W Smith, R Hope 1952*

Start at cairn 70ft R of Ithuriel's Wall. Climb small overhang to quartz-studded rocks and over steep slab to ledge (B); 6oft. Follow ledge on R to end, make TR across face to large block on Ardgartan Arete; 30ft. Climb direct then bear L to join original route; 50ft.

13.5 **Ardgartan Arete**

16oft grade IV+***: FA *J Cunningham 1948*

Start on S face and follow edge. Climb wall for 15ft to bulge, cross by mantelshelf into scoop, then TR diagonally L to join arete below large block. Climb arete to terrace (P); 9oft. Step out on wall to R and up two parallel cracks, then TR L to ledge, block B; 35ft. Climb crack directly above, B at top; 35ft.

15 **Ardgartan Wall**

200ft grade III**: FA *J B Nimlin, J Wynne, W Neilson, R Goldie 1937*

15ft R of Ardgartan Arete, climb direct up shallow groove; 6oft. TR R and upwards to grass shelf running across wall; 50ft. Climb wall to higher grass shelf; 20ft. Go direct up wall to finish on outcropping quartz; 4oft. Along grass shelf L, finish on steep wall beside overhang; 30ft.

15.1 **Chimney Arete**

9oft grade IV**: FA *J Cunningham, I Dingwall 1947*

Arete bounding R-angled Chimney on L. Arete climbed direct apart from one avoiding move about halfway, where short TR is made on R wall before rejoining arete.

15.C **Right-Angled Chimney**

10oft grade III**

Climb chimney direct to large overhang near top. Pass by L TR.

13 The Centre Peak of the Cobbler is to left of picture. Two climbers can be seen on path by-passing South Peak on the west

15.2 **Cat Crawl**

120ft grade v**: FA *A Lavery, another 1936*

Follow slanting fault L to R (hard). Fault goes into deep crack which splits face to R. From spike B TR outwards across lip of overhang on L wall and up to B. Move back to R and up short wall.

Direct Direct

105ft grade vi**: FA Upper Crack, *R Muir, J Wilson* Lower Crack, *J Cunningham 1948*

Follow main crack (middle section of Cat Crawl) and combine a direct ascent of lower crack with upper crack. Climb bulge L of recess to large hold, then up and R into corner; groove above climbed to spike B of Cat Crawl; 70ft. Climb awkward crack above B to top; 35ft.

15.3 **Club Crack**

100ft grade vi+***: FA *P Walsh, another 1954*

Climb to rock pocket. Continue up trending L to under overhangs, P runner. Up overhang slanting R in crack.

16.1 **Punster's Crack**

160ft grade iv***: FA *J Cunningham, W Smith 1949*

Start L of short chimney between Direct Direct and R-Angled Gully. Up and L for 30ft to crack in recessed corner, ascend wall to L of crack and cross ledges to B on L; 50ft. Move up and R to obvious gap. TR round bulge at far side of gap, follow ledge to R until further TR can be made diagonally L into crack. Follow crack to top; 110ft.

16.2 **Right-Angled Gully**

110ft grade ii: FA *Naismith, McGregor 1896*

Starts up obvious gully R of Punster's Crack. Follow gully (2 Pitches) to ledge below Direct Route. TR across R wall from ledge by inclined shelf to corner below short face. Climb face, take easy TR (L) by grass ledge to top of crag.

14 First Ascent of Porcupine Wall, near start of climb

Direct Finish
50ft grade IV* : FA *J B Nimlin 1930*
Start from top of second pitch R-Angled Gully, follow gully direct to top. This gives a hard winter line if iced up – very severe.

16.3 Right-Angled Groove
120ft grade IV+* : FA *J B Nimlin 1934*
Climb shallow groove lower and R of R-Angled Gully. Two bulges at 30ft and 90ft are passed by moves to L and climb finishes on grass ledge at exit of R-Angled Gully.

16.4 Echo Crack
120ft grade −V* : FA *J Cunningham, C Vigano 1949*
Start near L end of Halfway Terrace at big R-angled corner with crack. Up crack, 12ft and move into niche on L. TR L along loose ledge to crack in corner above Ramshead Gully. Up crack to top.

16.5 Incubator
250ft grade −V* : FA *J Cunningham, I Dingwall 1948* Lower Section, *J Cunningham, W Smith, T Paul*
Start just R of Ramshead Gully. Take a series of walls and traverses to Halfway Terrace; 130ft. Climb Echo Crack for 35ft then do rising TR R to grass ledges. Up ledges and finish by overhanging crack.

16.6 Recess Route
250ft grade III*** : FA *J B Nimlin, J Fox, R Ewing 1935*
Climb wall to grass ledges; 50ft. TR R to niche below bulge, climb to top of block; 25ft. Climb diagonal chimney to grass ledge below nail-marked chimney; 15ft. Climb direct to overhang at top, pass by TR to R, finishing at deep recess; 40ft. Up deep smooth-walled chimney to exit on L wall; 25ft. Scramble up ledges to grass terrace (Halfway Terrace), move 30ft R; 50ft. Move round at end of terrace into rock groove (the Fold) climb mainly on L wall, to overhung cave. Miss overhang by TR on R wall, or by easier route on L wall; 25ft. Climb cave on L wall to grass slopes; 20ft.

15 The North Peak of the Cobbler looking across to start of Right-Angled Gully (Left of 3). N=start of Right-Angled Groove

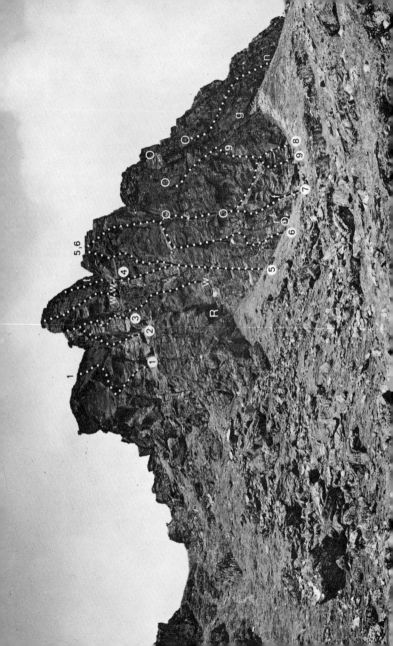

Note: Escape from the Fold (hardest pitch), without climbing down, can be done by TR L along Halfway Terrace to reach Ramshead Gully. The route can be very severe in winter and is a fine winter climb.

16.7 Fold Direct

140ft grade −v*: FA *J B Nimlin, R Browning 1936*
20ft R of Recess Route a fault runs to near top of cliff. Up vegetated crack to bulge, keep L until ledge is reached under deep scoop; 50ft. Up scoop to chimney with B; 60ft. Ascend chimney direct to edge of Halfway Terrace, to ST under Fold of Recess Route; 30ft. The fault line continues as the last three pitches of Recess Route.

16.8 Gangway

110ft grade IV+ : FA *Unknown*
Start 28ft R of N'Gombi and climb groove to under overhang of N'Gombi; 45ft. TR up and L up sloping fold and go round corner to join last pitch of Fold Direct; 65ft.

16.9 N'Gombi

150ft grade −v: FA *C Vigano, C White 1952*
Start 15ft R of Fold Direct. Go up awkward fault to middle of narrow fold slanting up R to L; 8ft. Go R, 15ft into corner under overhang, P. Swing R to ledge and B. Ascend rock above, keeping R of small chimney and finish over steep face. Easy ledges lead to top.

16.n North Rib

200ft grade III+*: FA *J Nimlin, J Fox 1935*
Climb steepest rock on rib: start 20ft R of Great Gully, with face climb, with L TR near top; 40ft. Continue up easy rock to scoop, climb this to ledge under crack; 50ft. Up crack, 8ft and TR L to steep rib, direct to rock ledge above Great Gully; 60ft. Easy to top; 50ft.

16 North Peak of the Cobbler. Circles denote climbers. Some of the boulders to left of picture are good howffs (shelter stones)

16.R **Ramshead Gully**

200ft grade III: FA *J and A Muir 1936*

Gully is easy for 80ft to foot of deeply cut chimney. Chimney climb to upper gully; 60ft. Short, boulder pitch (small holds); 15ft. Continue up gully, one step of jammed boulders; 50ft. This route can give a severe winter climb.

16.W **Wether Wall**

90ft grade V+**: FA *J Cunningham, H MacInnes 1951*

Start 10ft L of first rock pitch in Ramshead Gully. Climb wall 20ft and over bulge. Make difficult move to R, then L into shallow groove. Follow L wall of groove to overhang. Step L into second groove and finish on shelf below R-Angled Groove.

16.WW **Whither Wether**

120ft grade IV+***: FA *H MacInnes, W Smith 1952*

The shelf where this route starts is reached by a TR from foot of R-Angled Groove. Route is 15ft R of R-Angled Groove. Upward TR R to rock edge, step round to main face of Ramshead Wall. Climb wall, keeping close to edge, enter obvious recess. Finish by wall R of recess.

Variation

30ft: FA *W Smith, T Paul 1952*

Climb wall L of recess and follow edge to top of crag.

Glencoe Area, General

Going west towards Glencoe from Crianlarich there are easy but pleasant winter climbs on Ben Lui by the Central Couloir or the ridge to the left of the main snow Couloir. These are mentioned in the Route Descriptions and they can be fine excursions in good weather in winter.

With its easy access, Glencoe probably offers the best all round climbing in Britain; it has everything to offer from fine long rock climbs to excellent winter climbing. As a result of this the Glencoe section is the longest in this Guide.

Buachaille Etive Mor guards the eastern approaches to Glencoe, and this is one of Scotland's most popular mountains. With respect to summer not much need be said about the Buachaille, as it is known to Scottish climbers, but in winter, unless one knows the mountain it can be difficult finding one's way as the landmarks are often less obvious when covered in snow. See further details under 'Buachaille Etive Mor'.

Just short of the Buachaille, opposite Kingshouse West Roadend, is a road leading down to the Etive Slabs, some 14 miles on mainly single track road. Continuing westwards on the main road, at Altnafeadh, a deep corrie will be seen at the west side of the Buachaille (actually this peak of Buachaille Etive Mor is called Stob Dearg, 3345ft). This corrie, Coire na Tulaich, is the best descent from the peak and is also the walker's way up and the short gullies in its upper reaches can provide good sport in windy weather when it is not suitable to snow climb on the main peaks. At the foot of the corrie, across the River Coupall from Altnafeadh, is Lagangarbh Cottage belonging to the Scottish Mountaineering Club.

Running north from Altnafeadh is the Devil's Staircase, an old military road, which provides an easy start to the longer traverse of the Aonach Eagach as it rises to near Stob Mhic Mhartuin, the first peak. However, the Aonach Eagach is now more frequently traversed from a point three miles down the Glen. See 'Aonach Eagach Ridge'.

Continuing westwards, Buachaille Etive Beag (the Small Herdsman), is on the left with the valley of the Lairig Gartain on its eastern side and the Lairig Eilde on the west. On the west side of the Lairig Eilde is the first of the Three Sisters – Beinn Fhada – which provides a long, pleasant (and in winter interesting) ridge walk to Bidean nam Bian round two sides of the Lost Valley.

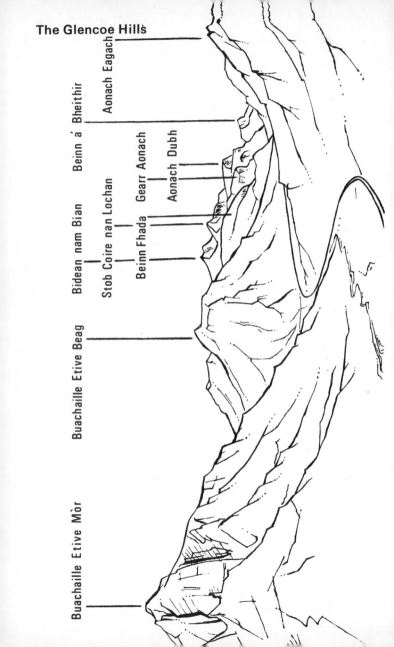

The Glencoe Hills

Aonach Eagach

Beinn a´ Bheithir

Gearr Aonach

Aonach Dubh

Bidean nam Bian

Stob Coire nan Lochan

Beinn Fhada

Buachaille Etive Beag

Buachaille Etive Mòr

The great wall of the Aonach Eagach Ridge is now visible, forming the north wall of the Glen, and opposite are the two remaining Sisters, Gearr Aonach and Aonach Dubh. Between Beinn Fhada and Gearr Aonach is the Lost Valley or Coire Gabhail, and between Gearr Aonach and Aonach Dubh, the Coire nan Lochan Valley, which leads up to Stob Coire nan Lochan.

On the other side of Aonach Dubh is the Bidean valley (Coire Beith), the stream from which flows into the River Coe, just below Loch Achtriochtan near the cottage of Achnambeitach. Directly above the waterfalls of the Bidean Coire, as seen from the road, is Stob Coire nam Beith (the Peak of the Birches), with Bidean nam Bian the highest peak in the area, 3766ft, round the corner to the left.

Forming the west sentinel of the massif is An T-Sron, with the deep cleft of the Chasm of An T-Sron immediately above. Left of the Bidean stream is the West Face of Aonach Dubh with its many clefts and buttresses.

A small road branches to the right at this point (the old road) and this too leads to Glencoe Village via the Clachaig Inn and the Youth Hostel. Above Clachaig Inn is Sgor nam Fiannaidh which is split at this point by the famous Clachaig Gully. This peak also forms the end (or the beginning) of the Aonach Eagach Ridge, unless one continues on to the Pap of Glencoe, Sgor na Ciche, 2430ft, which has a connecting ridge with Sgor nam Fiannaidh.

Most of Glencoe is the property of the National Trust for Scotland and there is no difficulty with climbing access at any time of the year.

Access
Being on the main road Glencoe is easy to reach. There is a daily bus service from Glasgow (usually change at Tyndrum) and a good British Railway sleeper service runs from Kings Cross to Fort William (for Glencoe there is usually a bus connection at Crianlarich). The road is seldom blocked except in the worst blizzards, and then only for one or two days at the most. To climb on the Etive Slabs, private transport is necessary as there are no public transport services down Glen Etive.

17 Overleaf: Ben Lui, Tyndrum, as seen from the approach track to the farm

All the climbs are within easy distance of the road and these routes should be clear from studying the photographs.

Camping/Accommodation
One can camp anywhere in Glencoe, but it is better to ask permission locally, as it can interfere with grazing and the movement of livestock. There are plans for at least one official camp site at the west end of the Glen. There are various hotels in the district: Kingshouse Hotel near Buachaille Etive Mor, which is also a skiing hotel, Clachaig Inn at the west end of the Glen and the Glencoe Hotel at Glencoe Village. There is also a Youth Hostel midway between Glencoe Village and Loch Achtriochtan on the old road. Beside the Youth Hostel is McColl's Bunkhouse which also provides accommodation for climbers and walkers.

Map: os 1 inch Tourist Map, Ben Nevis and Glencoe. This also covers Ardgour.

Guide Books: SCOTTISH MOUNTAINEERING TRUST: *Central Highlands* Campbell R Steven. *Glencoe and Ardgour* Volume I: *Buachaille Etive Mor* Volume II: *Glencoe, Beinn Trilleachan, Garbh Bheinn* L S Lovat. *Guide to Winter Climbs, Ben Nevis and Glencoe* Ian Clough

Mountain Rescue
Telephone 999 or Ballachulish 258. Rescue Post at Kingshouse Hotel, Achnambeitach and mobile unit.

1–4 Ben Lui

3708ft
From Tyndrum Station, take the footpath from E side to Cononish and continue past farm, to gain the lower slopes of Ben Lui. Routes 1–4 are easy winter access routes to summit (or descent). Route 3 is usually a straightforward snow climb (Central Gully). Route 2, the South Rib, is a narrow buttress directly below summit. The climb starts at lowest rocks and

18 Overleaf left: The summit of Ben Lui

19 Overleaf right: Stob a'Ghlais Choire as seen from the main Glencoe Road near Kingshouse Hotel. Sron na Creise on the right runs down towards Glen Etive

follows ridge. In summer it is about grade II–III, but it can be considerably harder in winter, though the start can be avoided by gaining the ridge above the difficulties from South Gully (the gully to L of the South Rib). South Gully is also straightforward.

19.1–3 Stob a'Ghlais Choire
3207ft

Access to this peak is from Black Rock Cottage on the ski tow road at the E end of Glencoe. Slant across moor round ridge of Creag Dhubh (small cliffs on L) and gain main basin of peak. Routes 1, 2 and 3 are all easy pleasant gully lines suitable for winter. Descend by first main coire on L to s of summit or traverse round ridge to Meall a'Bhuiridh (3636ft) and descend alongside ski tows. A=Access route. D=A descent route. The long buttress to the right of 3 also gives a pleasant winter route; take easiest line.

20.DGB D Gully Buttress
500ft grade III (Direct)* : FA *A Harrison, T Addenbrooke, L St Bartholomew 1929*

Start just L of D Gully. Climb buttress, then 6oft slab of rock with sloping holds. A grade IV route goes up R flank. (This rock slab can be by-passed on L via chimney). Follow on up 6oft on slabby rock to easier ground. *Winter* The route up the slab can be hard severe in winter and the usual line is the chimney to the L. (2–3 hours)** Standard–Difficult (2–5 hours).

20.CdR Curved Ridge
800ft grade I** : FA *G B Gibbs 1898*

This is main access route up mountain and provides an excellent introduction for the beginner. Route starts from top of the waterslab and keeps to L of Easy Gully passing under Rannoch

20 Buachaille Etive Mor, Glencoe. SS=Access path from main road at Jacksonville, from stepping stones, one mile east of Altnafeadh. L=Access path from Lagangarbh, by Altnafeadh. AR=Access route to Slime Wall and Raven's Gully (RG). T=Access route to East Face of North Buttress. WS=Waterslab. E=Foot of Curved Ridge. HL=Heather Ledge. CnB=Central Buttress. ct= Crowberry Tower. CfB=Cuneiform Buttress. GGB=Great Gully Buttress. S=Staircase Buttress. LB=Lagangarbh Buttress. Rannoch Wall is the left hand wall of CR (Crowberry Ridge).

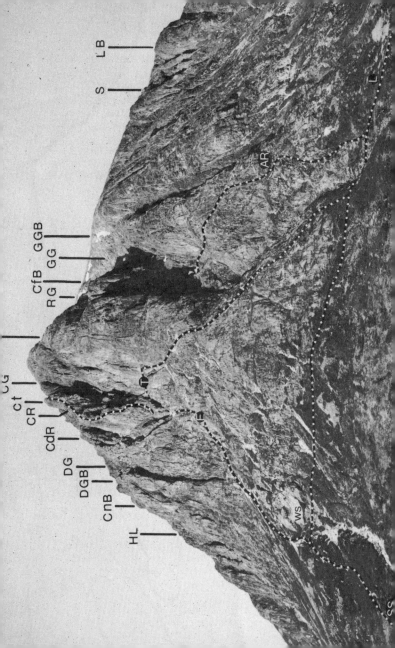

Wall to end below Crowberry Tower at cairn. From here easy scree gully leads round from L of Tower up to Gap, followed by short scramble up L past opposite top of Crowberry Gully to summit. In winter the Ridge can give an interesting though easy climb (not a good descent under snow).

20.DG D Gully

450ft Very Difficult–Severe (1½–4 hours)
Winter As a summer route this is not very interesting. In winter it can often give good sport, provided all pitches aren't banked over. Start from top L of waterslab in obvious narrow gully.

20.CR Direct Route, Crowberry Ridge

750ft grade IV***: FA *G D Abraham, A P Abraham, J W Puttrell, E A Baker 1900*

The original Direct Route by famous L TR from Abraham's Ledge. Start at R end of First Platform near Crowberry Gully at a 45ft pinnacle (not obvious) that abutts face (don't confuse with pillar lying against face at Fracture Route to L). Ascend shallow chimney on L side of pinnacle to Pinnacle Ledge, then a 15ft wall leads to Abraham's Ledge. Make an exposed L TR (sloping holds), then slant R and climb straight up to Upper Ledge, 40ft above Abraham's. (This Upper Ledge goes to R on to North Face.) From Upper Ledge TR L and upwards round corner. Route is obvious. Steep section ends with two long slab pitches (II). Easy slabs and narrow ridge lead in 250ft to base of Crowberry Tower (3000ft). Tower is climbed on N side, easy. Top is 3150ft. Descent of short side to Gap is 40ft, by an easy spiral descent from top. At base of Crowberry Tower a pathway leads from Crowberry Ridge round E flank into Easy Gully.

Variation to avoid L TR from Abraham's Ledge
(a) *Pinnacle Ledge* Moderate. From top of pinnacle 15ft below Abraham's Ledge, make R TR on to N face and return to crest by the Upper Ledge.
(b) *North Chimney* Moderate. From R-hand end of Abraham's

21 Buachaille Etive Mor in Winter. Even the easy summer routes can become hard in such conditions and plenty of time should be allowed for doing a climb.

Ledge descend short chimney, TR R and return to crest by the Upper Ledge.

Direct Route, *Winter*. FA *H MacInnes, C Bonington 1953* (5–10 hours). This route is always very severe when iced up and can be a major winter problem. The summer route was taken throughout.

20.CG Crowberry Gully, Winter

1000ft Very Difficult–Severe (2–11 hours)***: FA (Winter *W MacKenzie, J Russell, J Hamilton, J Dunn 9 February 1936* This route is described here for winter, and as such it is an excellent climb. In summer there are 8 principal pitches (IV) with a fork near the top giving two finishes. During a heavy winter all pitches can be banked-up but there can be up to five ice pitches. Crux usually is the TR R at junction of L & R forks. Above there is often at least one ice pitch and sometimes a P B on wall is necessary.

Left Fork, Winter Very Severe (extra 1–2 hours): FA (winter) *C Smith, R Taunton, I Robertson 18 March 1949* This finish, usually done in two pitches, is hard and crux is last section up iced capstone (keep L at top) and finish up easy ice corridor to Crowberry Gap. Two rock P sometimes required.

20.NB North Buttress

1000ft Severe (2–6 hours winter)**
This is the main buttress as seen in photograph of the Buachaille. It rises 1000ft from the base of the mountain to summit and, especially in winter, is a fine excursion. In summer, in recent years, it has been rather loose. (In summer grade II.) Best winter line is from bottom L where Buttress steepens in lower section, up chimney line towards the central chimney. From level with top of Raven's Gully the route is either up short chimney or to its L.

20.GG Great Gully

1200ft (winter) Difficult–Very Difficult (1½–2 hours)
On occasions in winter the gully banks-up and becomes little

22 Buachaille Etive Mor from the Glen Etive Road. LP=Lady's Pinnacle. ST=South Tower, Lady's Gully. CT=Crowberry Tower. cb=Central Buttress.

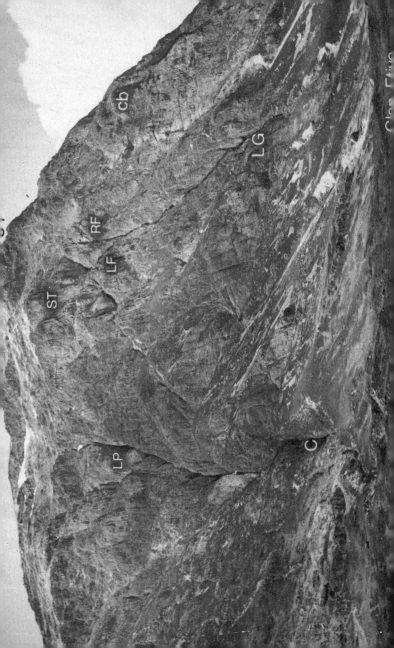

more than a walk. However, there are often two good ice pitches, the lower one (seldom in good condition) can give good sport. The other, below and to R of Raven's Gully, can sometimes be avoided. See route to Raven's Gully to avoid lower pitch.

22. LG **Lady's Gully**

800ft grade IV: FA *Mr & Mrs G Abraham 1900*

This route is situated R of the Chasm and just L of Central Buttress (CB routes not described in text). The Gully has 12 pitches and has been climbed by both forks near top. Climb up watercourse to where it steepens in long deep, grade III chimneys. Keep mainly to s walls for 200ft. Over scree to barrier wall of 150ft (escape routes). Climb 70ft up corner to R of watercourse by 2 steep chimneys; second is grade IV. Move L across chimney and round corner, make long L slanting TR across watercourse wall and climb narrow chimney of 30ft. Easy back to Gully. Climb corner above (crux) 80ft. Easy to Gully Fork.

22. RF **Right Fork**

Grade II: FA *W MacKenzie, J Dunn 1946*

R Fork is the direct continuation of Gully; climb 200ft of moderate rock to cave.

22. LF **Left Fork**

Grade IV: FA *D Goldie, R Goldie, J Dunn 1954*

Only difficulty is a 40ft pitch. There is also a cave pitch with various lines up it.

Winter Severe (4½–7 hours): FA *J Marshall, I Haig, G Ritchie* (by L Fork) *L Lovat, W Greaves* (by R Fork) *24 February 1957* Together with Clachaig Gully, the lower pitches of this climb are not often in winter condition. The route generally follows the summer line with usually a good ice pitch below Fork.

22. C **The Chasm**

1420ft grade −V***

Rock climbing starts approx. 20 min. from Glen Etive Road (1 m. s of Coupall Bridge). There are 16 main pitches with various escape routes up to Devil's Cauldron. Standard: generally about grade III and by easiest route at top (South Wall) grade −V. A fast party can reach Devil's Cauldron in

about $2\frac{1}{2}$ hours; almost another will be required to do the Direct, in dry conditions. These times should be at least doubled by an inexpert party. Main pitches in Gully are:
Pitch 4. Climb groove and crack between boulder and wall.
Pitch 5. Red Slab, a 9oft runout on L wall and above Gully forks; take R fork then ascend loose yellow wall, or the safer, easier groove going up R fork to watercourse. At its top move round to bed of Gully. Pitch 8. The Hundred Foot Pitch. Route goes up groove in corner on R of waterfall, grade IV; 95ft. Above, cross water to L wall and climb by R TR (Piano Pitch). The Converging Walls. Usually waterfall. Ascend to small ledge halfway up L wall and continue, straddling, facing gully then move to R wall. (This pitch can be avoided by ridge on L.) At Pitch 15, Devil's Cauldron, there are three routes:

The South Chimney
100ft grade −VI: FA *N Odell, M Stobart, Mrs Odell 1920*
This is the chimney on the L wall of Devil's Cauldron. Easy first 30ft. The chimney steepens and narrows, a ledge on R is reached. Climb for further 10ft, thereafter easier to finish. This is the hardest route of the three, but not so attractive.

The Direct Route
130ft grade V+ : FA *J Robinson, J Jack 1931*
This finish is usually wet. Ascend directly up watercourse to small cave and B (usually hard, wet and delicate just below cave). Chimney up, well out from cave, to reach prominent foothold on R wall. Good hold then in reach (crux section). Above are two small chockstones; after these the climbing is easier.

The South Wall
100ft grade −V: FA *C Allan, J H B Bell, Miss Roy 1934*
Ascend South Chimney for 25ft, B. Below B TR on to R wall round awkward corner and to good ledge. Take easiest line to top; 50ft.

Winter The gully, especially the lower reaches, is seldom in condition but when it is the Chasm provides an excellent winter

---

23 Overleaf: Rannoch Wall, Buachaille Etive Mor. 1. Top of Curved Ridge. Bottom left of picture is Easy Gully. Two climbers can be seen in Agag's Groove, (2). The start for Crowberry Ridge is just right of (3), up well-marked chimney

route. As mentioned in text, escape routes are available. Best time is during late February or March when there is more daylight; very severe (7–12 hours).

23.2 Agag's Groove

350ft grade IV***: FA *J F Hamilton, A Anderson, A C D Small 1936*
Climb up corner of wall beside rectangular block (just L of Grooved Arete). Up 90ft to B at start of groove. Short corner a little below block B is crux. Follow groove 110ft to B. Follow groove to easy L TR on open face beneath vertical nose. Up nose and L up to sloping top of block; 80ft. TR L and 75ft up face to ridge.

Winter severe***: FA *H MacInnes, K McPhail; C Bonnington, J Hammond, G McIntosh February 1953* (4–6 hours)
Crux was summer crux, P used for runner. Long moderate section was hard, due to ice covering holds. Second P runner used at vertical nose above large block B.

23.3 Grooved Arete

220ft grade −V**: FA *J Cunningham, W Smith 1946*
From groove beside edge climb straight up (small holds). Go L few feet and take B in Agag's Groove; 90ft. Climb R to arete, make delicate R TR (small holds) into groove. Slant R to last pitch of Fracture Route and Ridge.

23.4 Engineer's Crack

225ft grade V+ AI*: FA *H MacInnes, C Vigano, R Hope 1951*
Start Fracture Route and 20ft up TR L 13ft to small ledge in thin crack. Climb using some P to gain a point where it is possible to TR R to Fracture Route.

Direct Start: W Smith 1951 Climb crack directly from bottom, thus missing TR from Fracture Route; grade −VI

23.5 Fracture Route

225ft grade V+*: FA *K Copland, W Smith 1946*
Up pillar leaning against wall, 45ft to B. Climb the L fork of the V-shaped crack, 15ft (P), up further, harder section, 25ft

24 *Overleaf:* Rannoch Wall, Buachaille Etive Mor, Glencoe.
CT=Crowberry Tower. CR=Curved Ridge. EG=Easy Gully.
H=Haven. The black circle on Route 4 indicates climber. Route 13=Agag's Groove

(two mantelshelfs) to ST B. Finish R of upper nose of Crowberry Ridge. Or TR L round corner and up crack L of nose (harder).

24.1 Shattered Wall

190ft grade IV: FA *W Smith, H MacInnes 1952*
Start any part of wall between top pitch, Easy Gully and chimney on L of wall. Up 90ft to B well to L of obvious deep groove. TR horizontally R into groove. Go up this, until forced to go R round corner to easier rock, B; 90ft.

24.2 Wappenshaw Wall

230ft grade −V***: FA *W Smith, H MacInnes 1952*
Start at ledge above final pitch of Easy Gully, at steep corner. Up corner trending R until possible to move down R along obvious TR to block B; 90ft. Move R under big overhang to rib. Directly up under smaller overhang. Go 5ft L past detached block. Above are two steep grooves. Ascend, using both, then go L to shelf. Where it broadens, follow obvious fault up R to B; 110ft. Go back L and up short wall to top.

Variation to Pitch 2. FA *J R Marshall 1955* grade VI This straightens middle section of route. From top of pitch 1 of original route go up and L of big overhang and go up slanting R to grooves near top of pitch 2.

24.3 Peasants' Passage

230ft grade V+**: FA *W Rowney, H MacInnes 1952*
Between large red slab at Whortleberry Wall and final pitch of Easy Gully to L, is shallow corner. Climb corner 15ft, swing R to rib. TR slabs on R to narrow rock ledge. Go along R to ST P B; 50ft. Up round corner to steep wall with shallow crack. Climb to L (a few feet), then easier broken rocks to R, ST, B; 60ft. Above ST, slightly to R is steep corner. Climb it, 50ft to white rock spike. Go on to rib on R, continue to top.

24.4 Whortleberry Wall

390ft grade VI***: FA *J Cunningham, W Smith 1956*
Climb to B at 8oft (see photo). TR horizontally L 15ft, then gradually up to shallow groove, climb to small juniper ledge; 65ft. Immediately above are two thin cracks. Up L one for few feet, move to R. Easier climbing leads to B (ST of Peasants'

Passage). Make R horizontal TR for a few feet, then R upward TR to large grassy groove with overhanging top. Ten feet beneath overhang step R round corner and cross face R to small ledge B. Final pitch 120ft follows mossy crack directly above, easier climbing to large blocks.

24.5 Overhanging Crack

120ft grade −V: FA *B Nelstrop, G Byrom 1940*
Climb big red slab, 15ft L of initial chimney of Route 1. Up to spikes, above slab and close to chimney, B; 80ft. TR L into groove, up to 20ft crack (overhang at top). Up this and finish by 20ft wall above and join Route 1.

24.6 Route 1

230ft grade III: FA *G C Williams, G Todd, G G Macphee, I G Jack 1934*
Up short chimney to L of rock rib, B; 40ft. Slant up R, take long slant up narrow shelf to ST, two sloping slabs, and above, a 15ft wall. Up wall, or TR L round corner, and up. Finish up long upper groove.

Variation 24.7 It is possible to go up a groove and continue up line of least resistance to top. (IV approx.) See Route 8.

Winter Severe (2 hours) ***: FA *H MacInnes, A N Other February 1972*
The normal summer line was followed.

24.8 Red Slab

270ft grade V+***: FA *H I Ogilvy, Miss E Speakman 1939*
Route starts just above cave pitch in Easy Gully at overhanging corner. 30ft up groove, and easier 40ft to small ST B at bottom L of rock-nose. Move R round nose, TR ledge 20ft to juniper bush, climb a red slab (P). Do R TR round overhang, continue further

25 East Face, North East Buttress, Buachaille Etive Mor, CG= Crowberry Gully. BC=Bottleneck Chimney. NB=North Buttress. A good start for a winter ascent of North Buttress is by chimney line just right of traverse of Route 11. Circle indicates a climber on Route 4

20ft to corner, P runner. Crux is short vertical section above corner leading to easier rock B. Up 100ft to finish on the ridge about 15ft L of Agag's Groove.

24.9 Satan's Slit

260ft grade −V*: FA *H I Ogilvy, Miss E Speakman 1939*
Climb easy chimney L of large flake. Route slants R and runs at opposite angle to Agag's. It cuts across this climb. Follow up steep, easy rock to obvious flakes. TR L 20ft and up to R. B 100ft directly above start. Go 20ft, slanting slightly L, make TR hard R 40ft. This ends at Agag's Groove 40ft below nose. 15ft up Agag's Groove, move out R and up shallow scoop, go 30ft to P belay below overhanging crack. Up crack (crux), 30ft, easier for 30ft to top. Should crack be wet, finish to R.

24.10 January Jigsaw

250ft grade IV+**: FA *H I Ogilvy, Miss E Speakman 1940*
Climb directly up crack 25ft, halfway between a big semi-detached flake in Easy Gully and Agag's Groove. Then up L by 'stairs' to large flake. Go horizontally R along ledge to flake B above start. Go R and up by flake and wall, then directly to B below Agag's nose. From top of block B, TR R round corner into inclined groove. Up and right by groove passing the niche of the Haven (H) then gradually L up to P B under overhanging part of Satan's Slit. TR up R round corner into groove, up short way, then L onto steep wall. From top of this climb last 30ft of Satan's Slit to top, or easier groove to R.

24.11 Juniper Groove

150ft grade −V: FA *K Copland, C Lyon 1946*
Start about 20ft to R of big semi-detached flake, at a groove with a small sloping slab near the base. Up groove; 60ft. TR up L to small ledge. Step to R, round corner, make rising TR R and follow direct up groove to B (below Nose pitch of Agag's). Finish by Agag's.

24.12 Curving Groove

240ft grade −VI*: FA *J Cunningham, W Smith 1946*
Start 20ft L and above start of Agag's. The line is not obvious at start. Up with L trend to under overhangs. Two parallel breaks cut the overhangs (don't confuse with the deeper fault

to L, Juniper Groove). Ascend either break to gain common ST, B above. Up direct to Agag's Groove. There is a slab just above (faint arrow). Up slab by curving groove, then into wide exposed groove. This leads to the Haven (H). Finish by January Jigsaw and top of Satan's Slit.

25.1 North East Zig-Zag
155ft grade III : FA *P L McGeoch, H Grant 1940*
Go up L round corner on obvious long ledge to gain grass niche, then a short R TR up to grass ledge. Slant up R to big block on Slanting Groove, then L to Green Gully. Up to top of Gully to narrow obvious rib. Up rib, then R to follow up to High Ledge.

25.2 Slanting Groove
340ft grade IV : FA *H W Grant, P L McGeoch 1940*
10ft L of Shackle Route, under crack of Brevity Crack is a groove trending L. Continue to small ledge then directly up to B, easily turned on R. Straight up to Green Gully. 20ft below top of Green Gully, ascend crack, followed by black and slabby rock, slant R by steep rib to ledge below shattered overhang, avoided on L.

25.3 Brevity Crack
165ft grade —VI : FA *P Walsh, C Vigano 1954*
Approx. 15ft up wall and 10ft L of Shackle Route is a thin crack with small spike underneath. Go easily up to crack and harder up crack. Awkward mantelshelf to sloping ledge a few feet up crack (crux). Above, P B is level with sentry box of Shackle Route. Easier, though steep climbing to Green Gully.

25.4 Shackle Route
165ft grade IV** : FA *S H Cross, Miss A M Nelson 1936*
Climb crack 60ft, move on to L wall, (a few ft) to reach sentry box B. Move on L wall is crux. Continue up crack, easy rocks to Green Gully. Immediately above is tall pinnacle-flake with jammed block between it and L wall. Climb either black groove to R of pinnacle, followed by L slanting groove, a steep wall and easier rock to High Ledge or, climb up to and over jammed block to join the L slanting groove.

25.5 Shattered Crack

165ft grade —VI*: FA *J Cunningham, P McGonigle 1946*

A few feet L of Crow's Nest Crack and 3yds R of obvious wide crack of Shackle Route. Immediately L of V-shaped depression of Crow's Nest Crack go directly up steep wall passing large, loose flake. Locate small B below block overhangs well above, or TR L below these into sentry box of Shackle Route and B. Crack splits block overhang (crux is few ft of careful climbing; small holds). Steep climbing to Green Gully.

25.6 Crow's Nest Crack

285ft grade V+***: FA *J Cunningham, P McGonigle 1946*

Nine feet L of overhung recess, at V-shaped depression, go up 10ft, then slant slightly R 25ft to awkward step at corner, then TR R into narrow crack. Make a thin move onto slab on L 20ft up. Regain crack, where it is separated by overhanging nose. Follow up L crack to Green Gully. At bottom R of Green Gully, go up R to obvious crack from R of pinnacle-flake. Up 100ft to High Ledge.

25.7 Hangman's Crack

100ft grade —V+**: FA *R Donaldson, G McCarter 1941*

This is a very steep, clean-cut corner above Green Gully (grassy gully which cuts across the face). Ascend 30ft of easy rock to sloping ledge, B at base of crack. Up few ft slightly R to awkward mantelshelf move (crux). TR L into crack, follow until TR (—V) and long stretch is done onto R wall. Up steep rock to top.

25.8 Guillotine

95ft grade —VI: FA *W Smith, T Paul 1955*

From cairn, 30ft R of Garrotte, up overhanging wall with thin crack (P), to hard move onto small shelf; 25ft. L on groove above to top.

25.9 Garrotte

100ft grade —VI: FA *J Cunningham, M Noon 1955*

Up obvious crack, 10ft R of Hangman's Crack, for 70ft to ST (P runner at 40ft), no B. The 30ft section above ST includes an overhang, leading to easy ledges.

25.10 Mainbrace Crack

165ft grade —vi* : FA *P Walsh, W Smith 1955*
On the true east face, a few yards L of obvious chimney (Bottleneck Chimney) is a small overhung recess and conspicuous broken fault. Start at groove a few ft R of fault and climb overhang at 10ft and gain crack. 30ft up crack, then leave to TR up and L for 12ft to open groove. The groove leads to a L TR for 6ft to B. (This B is just above the upward step on Crow's Nest Crack.) Ascend wide crack above for 15ft then TR R to small ledge under an arete. Continue up arete to finish.

25.11 Pendulum

130ft grade vi+ : FA *P Walsh, J Cunningham 1955*
Start as for Gallows Route and 15ft under Gallows TR. TR L, 8ft to crack. Up crack and R side of small mossy slab onto sloping ledge. TR L to ST B; 65ft (P used on this pitch). Lasso big flake up R, swing and climb rope to mantelshelf onto flake top (loose). Up short way, TR across prominent chimney TR L (Bottleneck Chimney) and up fault on L wall to Green Gully. Note. This route has now been done without lassoing flake.

25.12 Gallows Route

130ft grade vi+** : FA *J Cunningham, I Dingwall 1947*
Go up chimney just R of corner for 40ft to B. Down 10ft, TR L 10ft to steep scoop (TR hard). Up scoop, climbing overhang on L, then a further scoop, turning further overhang on R by a shelf. Up third steep scoop to where L TR is made to better holds and ST and B. Easy to Green Gully.

30.CT Crowberry Tower, South Chimney (SC)

Summer Grade III : FA *J H Bell, J Napier, G Higginbotham 1898*
Winter, Mild–Severe : FA *H MacInnes February 1959*
Ascend obvious chimney from edge. Pleasant winter route.

26 *Overleaf left:* Rannoch Wall, Buachaille Etive Mor. The upper climber, (1) is on a higher belay than usual for Red Slab Route. The leader is approaching the harder section of the climb. (2) shows a climber on Agag's Groove, though the route is out of sight. (3) Indicates two climbers on Satan's Slit

27 *Overleaf right:* Whortleberry Wall, Rannoch Wall, Buachaille Etive Mor. The leader belaying at top of first pitch. The broken rock to right of him is Route 1

30.1 South Ridge

Grade II Winter Very Difficult: FA (winter) *N Tennant, H MacInnes February 1948*
Climb edge in two pitches.

31.1 Ordinary Route, Cuneiform Buttress

450ft grade IV*: FA *J H B Bell, A Harrison 1930*
From R end of grassy terrace climb short steep pitch and take easiest line by grassy grooves to further broad ledge below vertical upper third of buttress. TR R round corner onto W face. Climb obvious shelf, above which the route goes into centre of cliff.

Winter Severe (4–7 hours): FA *J R Marshall, D N Mill, G J Ritchie December 1957*
Summer route is followed throughout.

31.2 The Central Chimney

110ft grade IV+: FA *E Wedderburn, J H B Bell 1934*
A direct finish to Ordinary Route. From broad ledge below upper third of cliff, TR L to base of obvious chimney. Up vegetation, 50ft to gain cave, B. Continue on steep rock to top of buttress (rock rather unsound); 60ft.

31.3RG Raven's Gully

450ft grade −VI**: FA *J B Nimlin, B Braithwaite, N Millar, J MacFarlane 1937*
The approach to Raven's Gully is into Great Gully by route as indicated on photograph of Buachaille Etive Mor. There are eleven pitches, the longest being 65ft. Pitch 4 is crux; this is climbed on L wall. Pitch 5 has a large chockstone followed by an open groove above. Start of pitch 6 is on small holds on the

28 *Overleaf left:* Peasants' Passage, Rannoch Wall, Buachaille Etive Mor. At bottom right is the main Glencoe road, with the car park at Jacksonville

29 *Overleaf right:* Crowberry Ridge, Buachaille Etive Mor. The traverse from Abraham's Ledge

30 *Opposite:* Crowberry Tower and Gap, Buachaille Etive Mor. 2 shows climbers on easy access route to summit from top of Curved Ridge. Crowberry Left Fork exists from other side of Gap

L wall; this is longest pitch. Large arch rises above eighth pitch and above are caves of the Direct Finish. At top of pitch 8 a rib and shelf rises steeply on North Buttress side. Move L round foot of rib into grooves which are parallel with gully. Ascend about 150ft on easier ground to small platform on edge of gully, above finish of the Direct Route. Finish route by 10ft Corkscrew pitch, or by L TR across slabs and ascending short chimney.

31.3RG **Direct Finish**

Grade VI: FA *J Cunningham, W Smith, T Paul 1948*
Continue straight up gully at top of pitch 8. Ascend R wall then TR onto L wall to cave. After straddling, rocky shelves permit L-wards TR beneath large chockstones to grass ledge. Continue upwards to second last pitch of ordinary route. This finish is harder than the normal route.

Winter Very Severe***: FA *H MacInnes, C Bonington 14 February 1953*
Raven's Gully gives an excellent winter climb of very high standard. It is in condition during the winter more often than people realise, though pitch 4 (the crux) is seldom built up with snow. This was the crux in winter (two pitons); a further 3–4 may be necessary for B and runners. The last pitch and indeed the second last can be formidable.

31.4 **Guerdon Grooves**

540ft grade VI**: FA *J Cunningham, W Smith 1948*
150ft rope required. Start at cairn 20ft below Raven's Gully. Ascend series of grooves trending R to large flakes; 90ft. TR 10ft horizontally R round awkward square-cut corner to B. (If B not taken here run-out exceeds 150ft). Climb groove immediately above going slightly L; as soon as possible TR R into groove overlooking gully. Up groove. Route is difficult to find. Groove ends at projecting nose, and crack on L should be climbed leading to slab and so to small grass ledge with B and cairn. TR R across grassy corner into fault with overhanging top. Climb fault until easy TR can be made to B near Raven's Gully. Follow easy rocks 200ft to large terrace level with top of Raven's Gully.

31 Slime Wall, the west face of North Buttress (NB) and Cuneiform Buttress (CB). RG=Raven's Gully. GG=Great Gully

31.5 **Shibboleth**

550ft grade VI+***: FA *R Smith, A Frazer 1958*
Most direct line up cliff. Climb first pitch of Guerdon Grooves
to big flakes; 90ft. Up 20ft by crack on L, TR L 10ft and up R
to reach very obvious groove. Up groove, using P at 50ft, P B.
Continue up groove, step R at top and up L to B below flake
crack on Revelation; 70ft. Go up R 50ft to a jug-handle, TR L
for 10ft and climb to ST below L end of an overhang. Ascend
overhanging corner above and cross Girdle TR to B at 100ft.
Up and then L and gain shallow, overhanging corner, follow
to ledge on R and P B; 70ft. Final pitch 120ft. Climb wall
above, trend R by grooves to platform. Finish by overhanging
corner.

31.6 **Bludger's Route**

160ft grade VI**: FA *P Walsh, H MacInnes (alt. leads),
T Laurie 1952*
The first part of route is seen from any point near the foot of
Guerdon Grooves going straight up steep fracture to small rock
ledge below an overhanging section. Start at corner almost
directly below fracture and some 35ft L of and below Raven's
Gully. Climb to B below vertical section of fracture. Next pitch
to rock ledge (B), strenuous and sustained, occasionally overhanging. Up detached flake to R of groove, then step L into
groove. Up groove to rock ledge. Two P in position. From
rock ledge TR L along ledge. Go round corner, continue TR for
few feet, descend steep wall to base of large recess. Climb 20ft
chimney on L to reach terrace of upper tier.

Direct Finish: 100ft grade −VI: FA *J R Marshall, J Griffin,
G Adams, R Marshall 1957*
This finish connects Bludger's Route to start of Revelation.
Move L along rock ledge to corner, as described above. Climb
corner for 5ft, TR L into a vertical crack, follow this to ledge and
corner; move round edge to wall and climb on good slabby
rock, finishing by L move on to B of Revelation.

31.7 **Belial**

160ft grade IV: FA *J H B Bell, J R Wood 1940*
Climb is 6oft below foot of Raven's Gully. Climb 50ft slanting
L to grass ST. Take a direct line, enter R of two parallel 20ft
chimneys above. L chimney easier. Cairn above R chimney
marks end of route (below start of upper tier routes).

31.8 **Pluto**

160ft grade IV+ : FA *E Zenthon, B Fox 1940*

Start 15oft below base of Raven's Gully and level with big
detached block in Great Gully. Up 5ft to slab, TR L under
bulge and gain grass platform, 30ft. Up narrow 10ft chimney
to further grass platform, B. Up corner, then crack to triangular
ledge (crux); 40ft. This can be greasy and can be turned by
variation on R (IV+), finishing at same point. From ledge,
direct up short overhang and steep rocks to finish, or TR L and
up shallow groove, 80ft.

31.9 **Nightmare Traverse**

260ft grade VI* : FA *P Walsh, M Noon 1956*

The first pitch, 120ft, starts 15ft below Revelation. TR across
an arete then to L of small overhang; make awkward move R
round corner then across to flake, P B. Up rib above until TR R is
possible (hard) to small ledges; 120ft. Up crack 10ft then up
20ft to top of steep wall and small spike. Place P, descend
overhang using rope, to flake B. Up crack above, 20ft to small
ledge, B. Finish by Guerdon Grooves.

31.10 **Revelation**

290ft grade −VI* : FA *P Walsh, C Vigano 1956*

Above and R of Belial's finish is block B and easy R sloping
ledge. Follow ledge round corner, go up and R for few feet,
then L up steep groove to ledge; 100ft. B. Swing down from B
into steep groove, follow for 20ft. TR R to flake crack. Undercut
holds used on flake to swing into crack, up to poor ST, small
chockstone B below overhang; 80ft. Avoid this on L and up
40ft to B. Up 7oft to crest of large flake to R; easy to deep corner
with B at back.

31.11 **Doom Arete**

230ft grade VI* : FA *P Walsh, C Vigano 1956*

Ascend first pitch of Revelation. Return along ledge from B (a
few feet) and up steep wall trending L for edge and then up to
shallow corner. Start up corner, step L (crux) and follow to
ledge and above to small grass ledge, P B, 10ft above, 80ft
(exposed). Up to P, then by R TR round exposed corner to
crack, climb this to ledge, then a corner and on to finish.

31.12 **Bloody Crack**

130ft grade vi* : FA *P Walsh, S Crawford 1956*

From 25ft L of Revelation, at base of 130ft crack, climb crack 6oft to grass ledge (B 6ft L); strenuous. Re-enter crack and climb it to top.

32.d **Dalness Gully**

1200ft

Left Branch grade — vi : FA *J Cunningham, H MacInnes (alt. leads) S Jagger, C White 1951*

Central Branch grade — vi : FA *J Marshall, A Hendry, D Boston : L Lovat, T Weir 1955*

Right Branch grade vi : FA *D Whillans, H MacInnes 1959*

About 4 miles down the Glen Etive road opposite the cottage of Alltchaorunn (first cottage on L) is Dalness Gully. The Gully splits into three branches. The R fork is the hardest. The junction of the forks can be reached by R or L bank. There are few escape routes once committed to one of the forks. It is not possible to describe all the pitches. Start Gully a few minutes from road, or a short way up where it is drier. Above, a long pitch can be hard if there is a lot of water and higher still, where the Gully narrows, there is a short pitch which is climbed to L (on slab) of watercourse. Next pitch is long and quite hard; it goes up narrow rib L of watercourse then TR into Gully bed above waterfall. Next is a short hard cave pitch up watercourse. A long pitch leads to junction (easier descent to this is by N or true R bank avoiding lower pitches). The L Branch is the main Gully and the pitches in this are somewhat vegetated. An overhanging cave is climbed to R and the great barrier pitch is climbed to L (3 P runners). Three further pitches of (−v) approx. follow to top.

Central Branch : (c). This is entered by going up L Branch for short distance (beyond first bifurcation of R Branch). Under small boulder-pitch a corner leads R to base of Central Branch (Exit/entrance route to L bank is from above this pitch). Up water worn 6oft pitch above to gain L wall. Climb L wall by prominent cracked slab, overhang above. Climb steep corner,

32 Dalness Gully, Stob na Broige, Glen Etive. This Gully, which is close to the Glen Etive Road, is on the East Face of Stob na Broige, the southerly peak of Buachaille Etive Mor.

then L wall of same at 6oft. Up R to tree. TR R across wall and continue TR to pool (P at overhang). (—VI at overhang, also at tree pitch.) Climb pitch 4 on L or R wall. A series of pitches follow. Some distance above the Gully widens considerably and there is a continuation on L (grassy). True route is water-course on R to shelf above wall. Continue by long chimney on R to easier ground. Further pitches until gully opens out onto face of R wall (at cave higher up, water coming over). Up broken rocks to grey rock, following to L above cave. Easier pitches to top.

Note. It has been reported that loose rock makes this route dangerous at present.

Right Branch (r). This is the most difficult fork and the first few pitches are formidable requiring long run-outs, with little protection. About half-way the Gully slants up L with series of pitches to finish near rock pinnacle.

33.1 **Red Funnel Gully**

7ooft severe ($1\frac{1}{2}$–3 hours)**: FA *H MacInnes, R Baillie January 1964*

This route is easily reached from main road by the big cairn (see illustration). It is suitable when there is a heavy snowfall and higher routes are out of condition. The gully cuts the face of A'Chailleach and L branch should be taken. A 4oft pitch bars the way where R wall overhangs. Climb this and follow up main gully. It gets narrower nearer top. Return via summit, or TR out R into coire to E of peak and descend.

Note. As the gully starts low down, frost is necessary for a good climb.

33 *Opposite:* The Aonach Eagach Ridge from the east. E = Descent route to main road. B = Access routes to Am Bodach (B) and ridge. S = Start of path up the Lairig Eilde for Sron na Lairig

34 *Overleaf left:* In Red Funnel Gully, A'Chailleach, Glencoe. The main road is seen below

35 *Overleaf right:* The Aonach Eagach Ridge, Glencoe. The easy descent route (d) from the west end of the ridge comes down to the main road, just left of the bridge

Am Bodach

Aonach Eagach Ridge
3 miles (Winter) Difficult (6–10 hours)***

The Ridge is usually traversed from E to W starting at lay-by at Meeting of Three Waters. Start up true R of Allt-an-Ruigh and cross this some 200yds uphill and continue up side of stream, or take ridge to top of Am Bodach without crossing stream. The steep descent from Am Bodach can be one of the most difficult sections. On no account descend from the Ridge until the TR has been completed as a great number of accidents have occurred to parties doing so. Descent should only be down easy slopes leading to Loch Achtriochtan (see photo) or from the col between Sgor nam Fiannaidh and the Pap of Glencoe. In deep soft snow conditions the former route can avalanche. The path which follows the true R of Clachaig Gully though a good ascent route can be difficult to locate from above.

Note. Wind and snow conditions should be taken into account on this route.

35 Clachaig Gully
1735ft grade IV (30 pitches)** : FA *W H Murray, A M MacAlpine, J K W Dunn, W G Marskell 1938*. Winter, Very Severe (5–7 hours) : FA *H MacInnes, R Hope January 1952*

This climb is one of the most popular in Glencoe (it starts just above Clachaig Hotel) and is climbed to advantage in spring, when a profusion of wild flowers cover the steep walls. The climb is obvious as far as Great Cave Pitch, where the route goes right to a small tree growing from a crack on the rock face. From the tree a downwards, then horizontal TR leads to top of pitch. The short pitch following is probably crux of climb and above this, after short chockstone pitch, is Jericho Wall. This 70ft wall is to R of waterfall. There are several other good pitches above, the Red Chimney being the most significant. The best route for descent is by the west bank. There is a good escape route below the Great Cave Pitch up the west wall, through the small trees.

35.1 Farm Gully
800ft Very Difficult (2–4 hours)*

This is the obvious R branch of the wide gully, which runs up to crest of ridge. Start of gully is awkward, and the bottom few pitches, unless there is an unusually heavy snow fall, are best avoided up steep snow slope on L with some tree B. Several ice pitches. If this route is done during sunshine there can be a danger of falling stones.

35.2 Twenty Minute Gully

600ft Winter Difficult*: FA *H MacInnes, Party February 1969*
This is first obvious narrow gully down from crest of Ridge below steep step to W of Am Bodach. Gully curves L and provides an excellent means of gaining summit when TR Ridge from W to E.

35 Vice Chancellor Ridge

700ft Winter Very Difficult (2 hours)**: FA *H MacInnes, Party February 1969*
This is obvious ridge just L of Big Chock gully. Ascend directly up ridge from snow slope to first rocky tower. Continue in two rope lengths to more formidable tower, take central line. Above a rocky wall is climbed to gain top of further more exposed tower. TR narrow snow arete at rear to easier ground. Reach a steep step in ridge in a further rope length. This can be climbed direct (slightly to R of centre) severe, or take easy gully on R to reach easy ground leading to summit.

35.bc Big Chock Gully

700ft Winter Severe (2–3 hours): FA *H MacInnes February 1960*
This route is the obvious gully to L of Chancellor Buttress. The main difficulty is surmounting the big chockstone pitch halfway up. This is climbed on R wall on ice; seldom in condition and requires a very big build up of snow and ice.

35.3 The Chancellor

1000ft Winter Severe (3–4 hours)**: FA *W Skidmore, R Richardson December 1965*
There are two starts to this route, a shallow snow gully which runs up into buttress or the ridge to R. There can be difficulty route finding on this climb, especially in steeper middle section where it is better to keep L.

35.om Old Man Gully

900ft Winter Very Difficult (1–3 hours): FA *H MacInnes February 1960*

This prominent gully gives a good climb to summit of Am Bodach in heavy, hard snow conditions. The gully can be entered from L and some of the lower pitches can be by-passed. Various exits at top, which can be sometimes steep and corniced. Access to gully base is up scree/snow slope from main road directly below col to w of Am Bodach, towards low point on ridge. Keep to true R of small stream on approach.

38.2 **Sron na Lairig**

1000ft Winter Difficult (1–3 hours)***: FA *J Black, C Montgomery, Miss A Williamson, Miss R McCulloch November 1949*
An obvious ridge bounding the E side of Coire Eilde, which is the true source of the Allt Lairig Eilde. The lower part has much variation, but above the route is well defined. A prominent block marks the beginning of the crest. Then the ridge is narrower and often icy.

40.1 **The Midge**

400ft Winter Difficult (1 hour): FA *H MacInnes and party February 1969*
Follow crest of buttress starting to L of Wasp. It is possible to finish via Gully A from wide snow ledge.

36 *Overleaf left:* On the Aonach Eagach Ridge. Glencoe in winter

37 *Opposite:* Lost Valley (LV), Gearr Aonach and Aonach Dubh, Glencoe. 1 and 2=Access routes (see Lost Valley photographs). 4=Access route to Beinn Fhada up gully (out of picture). Alternative route is from waterfall at gorge up NE nose of Beinn Fhada to gain summit ridge. Note. It is essential if descending this way in winter to keep to east of the nose. 3 and 5=Access routes to Stob Coire nan Lochan. ZZ=Zig-Zag up Gearr Aonach (access to Stob Coire nan Lochan). N=The Nose of Gearr Aonach. E=East Face of Aonach Dubh. LVB=Lost Valley Buttress. R= Start for Aonach Eagach Ridge up true R bank of stream

38 *Overleaf right:* Sron na Lairig, Glencoe. This ridge is usually reached from the Glencoe road from the gorge or footpath starting opposite the big cairn at the signpost indicating the footpath to Glen Etive through the Lairig Eilde. 1=A short steep gully (Severe). An easy gully up to the arete of Sron na Lairig. A climbing party is visible at start of route mark

40.2 **Beinn Fhada,** West Face
The Wasp

400ft Winter Hard Severe (4 hours)** : FA *A Fyffe, C MacInnes, A Laing, J McCattan, R Sherman*

This climb is on the buttress to L of main summit, see photograph. Ascend a narrow twisting chimney for 2 pitches with hard moves at top of each pitch. Continue easily to top of buttress.

40.3 **The Cleg**

400ft Winter Very Severe (1 hour) : FA *H MacInnes and party March 1969*

This climb is to R of Wasp and follows a diagonal line running from near start of Wasp on rock wall. Crux is narrow hanging scoop, 2 P. Continue up buttress to summit.

40.4 **Broken Lip Gully**

580ft Winter Very Difficult* : FA *I Clough, F Jones and party February 1969*

Follow chimney/gully line from L side of buttress, from snow bay to top. It runs just parallel to Main Buttress.

40.5 **Beinn Fhada,** NW Face
Main Buttress

700ft Winter Very Difficult (1–2 hours)* : FA *H MacInnes, D Lane-Joynt February 1969*

Take a direct line up buttress, going slightly R after first pitch to ascend short snow gully. Break L to buttress, various lines to top.

39 Opposite: On Sron na Lairig, Glencoe. Route 3 exits at this point

40 Overleaf left: The West Face of Beinn Fhada from the Lost Valley. B=Gully climb of Moderate standard. Best approach to this buttress is up from L end of Lost Valley flat section, directly up to lower rock buttress on left of picture. Best access to the main buttress on right is by the true left side of gully G, from true right path up Lost Valley

41 Overleaf right: Bidean nam Bian and the head of the Lost Valley. BD=Bealach Dearg. BL=Stob Coire nan Lochan, Bidean, Bealach. Easy continuation of Gearr Aonach ridge to summit

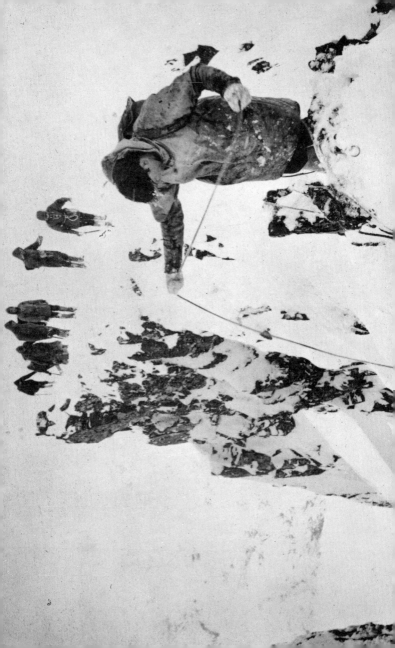

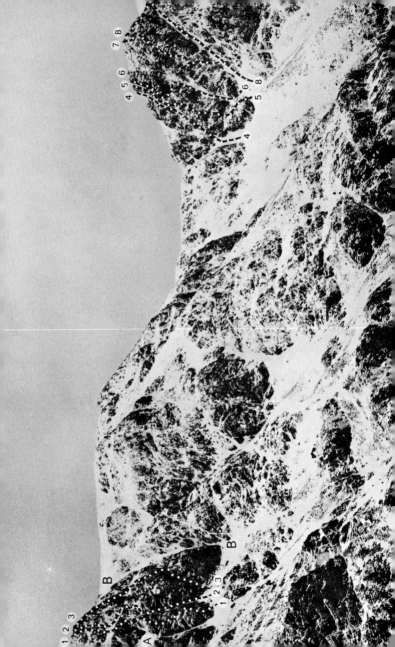

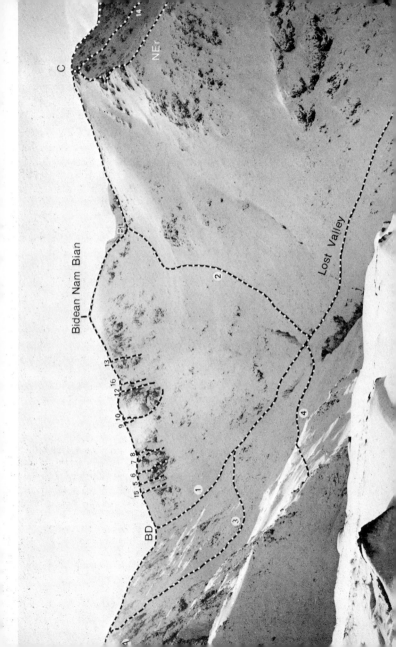

40.6 **Twine Climb**

600ft Winter Very Difficult (1–2 hours)*: FA *J MacArtney and party February 1969*
Go up chimney scoop line and TR L along snow to take parallel line to Main Buttress to top.

40.7 **Quintet**

440ft Winter Hard Severe (1 hour)*: FA *H MacInnes, D Chen, R Birch, P Judge, R O'Shea 1969*
This climb follows the snowy corridor, which cuts diagonally across the face from L to R. Start from ramp going directly up iced chimney to block B; 70ft. Continue up to narrowing section of gully and bridge up and R over edge to gain the true corridor. An awkward section 70ft above leads to easier ground, continuing up corridor to near top of buttress.

40.8 **The Ramp**

700ft Winter Difficult ($\frac{3}{4}$–1 hour)*: FA *H MacInnes March 1949*
Follow line up ramp, then to crest, then up to summit.

Winter Climbs

1. Descent route from head of Lost Valley, sometimes small cornice.

2. Descent route from Bidean/Stob Coire nan Lochan Bealach. Keep to line indicated on descent as waterfall pitch, visible just above junction of routes, is dangerous.

3. Easy face route up Stob Coire Sgreamhach, A (3497ft).

4. Access route to col at bottom section of Stob Coire Sgreamhach summit ridge.

5, 7, 9, 10, 14, 15, 16. All winter gully climbs of up to Difficult standard.

6. *Chimney Route* 240ft Very Severe (1–2 hours): FA *R Marshall, J Moriarty, January 1959*
This climb follows a very prominent chimney splitting corrie face of buttress. This gives a series of problems over icy chock-stones.

8. *Granny's Groove* Severe: FA *H MacInnes and another January 1960*

---

42 Lost Valley Buttress, Glencoe. Looking across to Stob Coire Sgreamhach (A), which forms the corner peak on the Beinn Fhada/Bidean Ridge. Routes 1,2,3,4, are those described and numbered on other Lost Valley photograph. 6 = Chimney Route. b = Easy gully to top of Lost Valley Buttress. 9 = Right-Hand Gully. BD = Bealach Dearg

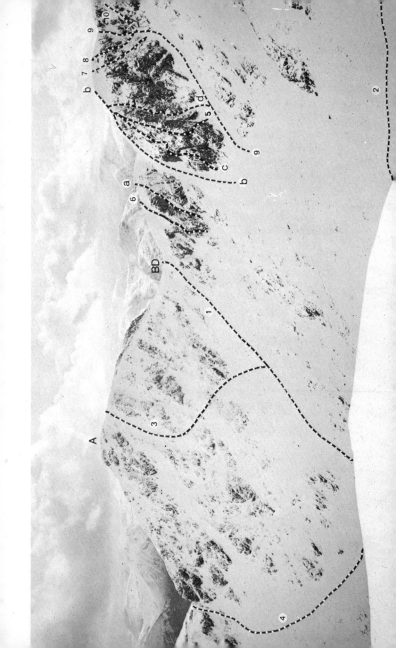

This is the R branch of 7. Go up steep corner scoop sometimes with overhang, turned on L.

12. *Right-Hand Gully* 200ft Difficult** A pleasant gully climb sometimes giving an ice pitch above a cave. Usually cornice at top.

13. *Short Gully* 100ft Difficult The narrow chimney/gully to R of easy snow couloir. Sometimes an ice pitch at top.

42.a Right Edge

300ft Winter, Severe (2–3 hours)** : FA *J R Marshall, J Stenhouse, D Haston February 1959*

Take broad snowfield ramp on R of face which runs up R under overhangs. The ramp is gained by chimney, below L side. From top of ramp take the arete to ridge.

42.c Sabre Tooth

400ft Winter, Hard Severe (2–3 hours)** : FA *I Clough, H MacInnes (alt. leads) February 1969*

Go up right into snow bay, B in corner. Go out R to edge then up to terrace (easy route off L along ledge). Go L along terrace to steep corner, B. Up corner then R along ledge to B. Follow chimney/grooves to top.

42.d Pterodactyl (Moonlight Gully)

350ft Winter, Very Severe (3–5 hours)** : FA *H MacInnes, D Crabb January 1964*

Go directly up to obvious overhanging entry, which forms the bottom of steep chimney line on upper section of buttress. The entry into the upper chimney is the crux.

42.5 Tyrannosaur

400ft Winter, Very Severe (2–4 hours) : FA *I Clough, T Winkler, D Morrish, S Taylor March 1969*

This climb takes the well defined R edge of the L section of cliff, starting on R wall well below corner of Pterodactyl and some 30ft up from lowest rocks. Start up short shallow chimney and follow thin crack continuation which trends slightly L and over buttress edge to reach snow bay. The line looks improbable from base and is sustained (good protection). From snow bay a steep corner crack is followed up to L of crest (initially using slings for aid, hard and sustained). Final section of climb gives two long pitches of easier climbing by steep snow grooves close to crest.

42.7 **Dislocation**

280ft Winter, Severe (2–3 hours) : FA *C J S Bonington, F Mitchell 1969*

This climb is on R-hand side wall of buttress and leaves the Gully about 50ft above the toe of buttress. A groove line which trends slightly R is followed to snowpatch above which a shallow broken chimney leads to top.

42.8 **Trilobite**

200ft Winter, Very Difficult (1–2 hours)* : FA *I Clough, H MacInnes (through leads) February 1969*

Go up steep groove from a point where Right-Hand Gully starts to narrow. Climb to top trending L on upper part.

42.10 **Snow Ramp**

300ft Winter, Difficult: FA *H MacInnes February 1949*

Go R up obvious ramp to R of Right-Hand Gully.

47.A **Gully A** (Right Fork)

800ft Winter, Very Severe (4–6 hours)** : FA *H MacInnes, D Crabb January 1964*

Reach gully proper up steep initial pitch, either direct or on the L. The route above, where the gully steepens is obvious, keeping to the R up steep ice scoop then up ice bulge in chimney, P B above. Follow on up true gully bed to top.

47.LL **Lost Leeper**

600ft Winter, Severe (2 hours)** : FA *H MacInnes, A Gilbert, P Debbage, D Lane-Joynt, D Allwright*

This is next definite snow/ice chimney line to R of Gully A and skirting L edge of E face of Gearr Aonach. Take line of approach (in winter) as shown in photograph and ascend narrow ice chimney to L of main face. After a rope length break out L to gain further ice chimney and ascend this and continuation to bay below steep ice pitch (small tree B). Climb ice pitch direct and remaining pitch to top. Mainly P B throughout.

45 Overleaf left: Lost Valley, Glencoe, Gully 7. Granny's Groove is in the foreground

46 Overleaf right: The steep ice pitch on the Wabe, above the icicles. The route goes up and right on the ice above climber

47.1 **Rainmaker**

200ft grade IV+***: FA *R Marshall, J Moriarty 1958*
L edge of the face is a deep recessed diedre. Ascend this. There
are a few overhangs (good rock).

47.2 **Mome Rath Route**

310ft grade IV**: FA *J S Stewart, Mrs M Stewart, Miss C Stewart
1954*
L of a spring on broad shelf a prominent line on a grey shelf of
rock leads L; 80ft. Climb light grey rock trending L to flat grassy
perch at foot of steep exposed chimney on L of big overhangs
well up cliff. Chimney above goes to top of wall. Exit L at top.

Winter 47.a
450ft Very Severe (4½ hours)***: FA *A Fyffe, J McArtney
February 1969*
Follow summer route to base of first chimney; climb this till it
fades out at approximately 60ft. Make a L TR into another
chimney. Climb this for short distance to a bay on L. Climb a
slabby ice plated rib on L leading to a short steep corner
chimney (a) at top of cliff.

47.3 **The Wabe**

300ft grade IV***: FA *J Brockway, J B Baxter, J S Orr 1954*
Just R of Mome Rath Route is a cairn. Up to ST by flake and
groove, to under small overhang. Go L to slab, then R to ST and
B in corner. TR L onto wall and up 100ft to big block. TR R then
up recessed rock, immediately R of big overhangs to gain ST
on rib on R. Go L to slab on top of overhang and directly up
wall to top.

43 Opposite: The steep corner on Sabre Tooth, Lost Valley
Buttress, Glencoe

44 Overleaf left: Lost Valley, Glencoe. The cornice exit on Right-
Hand Gully

47 Overleaf right: The East Face of Gearr Aonach beyond Rev. Ted's
Gully (RT, with variations D, d). This face is situated above the
Lost Valley path, beyond the flat section of valley floor

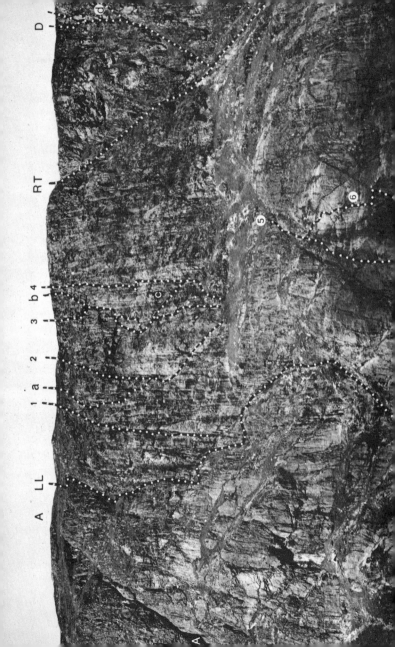

Winter 47.bc
Very Severe (2–4 hours)*** : FA *I Clough, H MacInnes, J Hardie February 1969*
Route follows ice fall more or less in line of summer route about 75ft R of Mome Rath. Up 20ft wall to snow ledge. Then up rock and ice making L to small ST and flake B 10ft below prominent nose (150ft). Pass nose on L then up R and L to B on block of summer route; 70ft. Follow summer route up recessed panel to ST on rib; 50ft. Go R and up then L and up to top in 150ft. Start at c and finish at b.

47.4 **Mimsy**

300ft grade IV* : FA *I McFadzean, H Noble 1960*
Close to R end of wall above broad shelf is a R inclined grassy groove. 20ft R is a crack (start of route). Above crack ascend broken rocks to grassy ledge (nearby bushes). Follow line of shallow gully and exit L where exposed crack is seen. This leads to broken ledges. Up crack, continue by these ledges and steep 60ft rocks to top.

47.5 **Slimcrack**

160ft grade —v : FA *I Clough, C G M Slesser 1965*
The thin vertical crack, hard at halfway, then slabs and scrambling to top.

47.6 **Flake Groove**

240ft grade IV : FA *I Clough, G Brown, J G Donnison, R A Logan 1967*
Climb diagonal crack-groove past large pinnacle-flake to ledge and B; 90ft. TR L across wall and up to small ST and thread B; 30ft. L and up slabs and wall to B; 120ft. Scramble to top.

48 Opposite: Gully A, Gearr Aonach, Glencoe. Looking down to the piton belay above the difficult section in gully, on the first ascent

49 Overleaf: First Ascent of Mome Rath Route in winter. The leader can be seen on the slabby ice plated rib on the left. Photograph taken from The Wabe

50.4 **Chancellor Gully**

1700ft Winter, Very Difficult (2–4 hours) : FA *H MacInnes and party 1960*

In icy conditions this Gully can be quite hard, but such conditions are not frequent. It is best to enter Gully from true L bank into junction, below the Slit. The Gully can be finished by Glenmore Gully (5) or continue on up.

50.S **The Slit**

400ft grade V+ : FA *H MacInnes, M C MacInnes 1962*

This is the obvious chimney rising from Chancellor Gully. Gain chimney from crack continuation below and follow on up into chimney. Climb in two pitches to exit on shelf at top R.

50.5 **Glenmore Gully**

500ft Winter, Very Difficult (4 hours from road)* : FA *H MacInnes, B Hall February 1963*

Ascend Chancellor Gully or true R edge to gain overhanging start of Glenmore Gully. Turn this up L then R. Up gully to large chockstone, climb wall to R and up into gully above. Finish up steep partly enclosed scoop to top.

50.6 **John Gray Buttress**

900ft Winter, Very Difficult (2–4 hours) : FA *H MacInnes and party 1959*

Take a line close to Ingrid's Folly to steeper rock. Take easiest line up snow scoops with several TR. At definite chimney go up, then L and slant R to steep step. Climb this direct. Continue up gully (tree B on R) and go R to gain edge of gully to top, or continue up gully line up steep pitch (severe) and on to top. Only suitable after heavy snow fall, followed by frost.

50.7 **Ingrid's Folly**

900ft Winter, Difficult (1–2 hours)*

This route, together with the others on this lower part of this

50 Previous page: Part of the East Face of Gearr Aonach with the Aonach Eagach Ridge behind. E=Easy routes on Ridge. 1=Farm Gully. 2=Vice Chancellor Ridge. 3=The Chancellor. T=Traverse line. LV=Lost Valley. Z=Zig-Zag route up Gearr Aonach. Note. In sunshine the routes on East Face of Gearr Aonach are subject to stone/ice fall

face are suitable when the snow line is low and conditions are poor on the tops. Various pitches to top including a through route. In heavy soft/thaw snow, this route is subject to avalanche conditions.

50.8 Peregrine Gully

500ft Winter, Difficult (2 hours)* : FA *H MacInnes and party 1959*
Take Ingrid's Folly to above through-route, then TR up L into shallow gully line. There is one pitch before open snow slope leading to big chockstone. Turn this on L and follow up to under the great chockstone to top. It is also possible to finish last proper pitch of Ingrid's Folly (L TR pitch) and go horizontally L over mixed ground to gain Peregrine below great chockstone.

50.9 McArtney's Gully

500ft Winter, Mild Severe (1½ hours) : FA *H MacInnes and party February 1969*
Approach from Ingrid's Folly and Peregrine, or from lower reaches of Rev. Ted's Gully, or direct (see illustration). Ascend corner for several pitches to where gully steepens. Head for narrow rock chimney near centre and climb this and short groove above. Break out L either by ascending snowy ramp or L along TR to gain L corner.

50.a Frostbite Wall

680ft Winter, Very Severe (2 hours)** : FA *H MacInnes, A Gilbert, P Debbage, D Lane-Joynt, D Allwright February 1969*
This route takes line of obvious ice fall up main face between Rev. Ted and McArtney Gullies. Initial section is climbed to R of ice fall. This is crossed at ledge with small tree and bulging section of ice fall climbed either direct or to L (good B). This climb is usually in condition when ice fall is full length of face.

50.10 Rev. Ted's Route

11,12   1000ft Winter, Severe (4 hours)** : FA *H MacInnes, another 1959*
This gully is suitable when the snow line is low. The line of the gully is followed to the main fork. Direct route goes straight up in line with lower gully, but starts L up chimney, then out R then up, then L again. This finish can be severe. The R branch of the R fork provides the easiest route and is generally easier than the lower gully (difficult). The chockstone finish, ie the

L branch of the R fork is the hardest and goes up direct under chockstones, P B. Flake B under second chockstone. Last pitch can be done straight up steep iced crack or L to easier ground, then up R (thin P useful for some B). Severe.**

53.1 **Herbal Mixture**
200ft grade IV : FA *J R Marshall, G Ritchie 1957*
From a shallow bay below L end of prominent overhang, go up vegetated grooves to B; 40ft. Up on cleaner rock above to B under steep top wall; 70ft. Up wall by L slanting line to top; 90ft.

53.2 **The Mappie**
250ft grade V+* : FA *J Moriarty, J R Marshall 1959*
From rear of shallow bay climb crack leading to L end of prominent overhang; 60ft. TR L, 20ft, and up to easier ground; 70ft. Finish by steep wall above; 120ft.

53.3 **Marshall's Wall**
250ft grade VI** : FA *G J Ritchie, R Smith 1960*
Start from below a small bulge and well to R of a curving line of overhangs. Ascend L then back R above bulge to spikes. Go R, then up, then R again to small ledge. Up L to ledges and finish up undercut corner.

53.4 **Bunny's Route**
320ft grade III+ : FA *H MacInnes, Mrs T Laurie, Miss A Williamson 1952*
Start from up L of start of Zig-Zag and climb to ledge below the short, wide, deep chimney of the route. A fault leads to this by a L slanting line. Up fault and chimney in three pitches.

Winter, Severe (2–3 hours)
Though not often in good ice conditions it can provide a good short winter climb starting from the ledge below the fault.

51 *Overleaf left:* The Central Branch of Rev. Ted's Gully, the chockstone pitches

52 *Overleaf right:* The Great Chockstone, Peregrine Gully, Glencoe

53 *Opposite:* East Face of Gearr Aonach, Glencoe. This face is just L of Zig-Zag, Z-Ž-Z. Circles mark climbers

54.1 **The Cheek**

350ft grade v** : FA *H MacInnes, M C MacInnes 1968*

Start is common with Prowl. Start up easy rock leading up R near small watercourse and work L towards rowan tree on grassy ledge above. B on rock below this. Climb to rowan tree ledge and continue along to chimney and climb into small bay few feet up, B. (The Prowl continues straight up chimney.) Move L round steep corner and diagonally up L to small ledge on edge of wall. TR round to L of this horizontally and down, across to and up grove to block B above; 65ft. Climb chimney above direct to B on ledge; 6oft. Finish on L on easy wall of fine rock.

54.2 **The Prowl**

250ft grade IV+** : FA *D Haston, J R Marshall 1959*

Approx. 100ft L of the R end of the obvious ledge, there is a recess past a large rowan tree. Ascend 10ft up chimney above to small bay and B. Leave bay by a crack and follow direct line to top.

54.3 **The Walk**

26oft grade IV** : FA *J R Marshall, R Marshall 1959*

Take a diagonal line L up two grass bays to top of face. Finish by Prowl.

54.AB **Avalanche Gully**

1000ft Lower Left Fork – Very Severe, Upper Left Fork – Very Severe, Original Route – Very Difficult : FA *H MacInnes and parties* (Lower Left Fork, winter ascent unrecorded)

This gully starts just above access path to Stob Coire nan Lochan. It is only suitable during heavy snow conditions, followed by a short thaw and freeze up. The Lower Left Fork can give a hard climb though short, finishing on open ledge exiting L. Original Route goes up R at this junction, up steep ice pitch (can be turned up R wall) to reach easier section. Above, a further short pitch, climbed on R is followed by a longer pitch to narrow part above. Go up L past tree and follow gully to fork. The Upper Left Fork starts in a short pitch and

54 The North Face of Gearr Aonach, Glencoe. a=Access route from bridge over the River Coe. The skyline ridge to the left gives a pleasant route (grade II) to the top. This is right of the Zig-Zag

goes on up under big chockstone to steep pitch (seldom in suitable condition). Above a further pitch, usually climbed on L leads to easier snow and top. If this Fork is not in condition, it is possible to go R from below through section, onto easy buttress and join original route above. An escape route L is also possible from under through route. Original Route goes up R of fork, then back L up steeper iced rocks to easier slopes to top. When descending the Zig-Zag in winter ensure that the correct line of descent is taken. A cairn at top marks start-down face towards The Meeting of the Waters: slant down L under small wall. Down to next cairn directly below. Down easy gangway/ chimney slanting L, make long TR back R along big terrace to rowan tree above short step. Down step and back L along big long terrace (between the two main walls) until, at end, a chimney goes down to heathery/snow shelf. This is taken back R under steep wall to trend down L to easy ground.

57.F Farewell Gully

500ft Winter, Severe (2–3 hours)* : FA *J McArtney and party February 1969*
This gully is obvious from the high path to Stob Coire nan Lochan. There are a number of steep short pitches. Route can be hard if there is a poor build up of ice.

57.1 Ciotach Route

300ft Winter, Very Difficult–Severe (1 hour) : FA *H MacInnes and party January 1959*
Go L from 999 approach and gain icy section rising to ridge. Variation possible.

55 *Overleaf left:* The fine upper section of The Cheek, Gearr Aonach, Glencoe. Below is the Old Glencoe Road and the River Coe

56 *Overleaf right:* Looking down to the through route in Avalanche Gully on Gearr Aonach, Glencoe

57 *Opposite:* The West Face of Gearr Aonach from the summit of Aonach Dubh. Beyond are the gullies on West Face of Beinn Fhada, across the Lost Valley. 6 = The Wasp. 7 = The Cleg. 8 = Main Buttress. 9 = Twine Climb. 10 = The Ramp. The Stob Coire nan Lochan path goes up the valley in the foreground on the true right of the stream

57.2 **Rescue Team Gully**

250ft Winter, Hard Severe (2–3 hours)*: FA *H MacInnes and party March 1966*

This is the very steep short gully directly ahead as you approach. Ascend iced chimney.

57.3 **Jim's Gully**

320ft Winter, Severe (1 hour)*: FA *J McArtney and party March 1968*

This starts as for 999 or more direct up from L of start of this route. Follow curving line of gully to top.

57.4,5 **999**

400ft Winter, Hard Severe (2 hours)***: FA *H MacInnes, G Kyniston, Miss G Marshall, J Friend February 1969*

This is the R of the three gullies. Take R fork at junction and ascend to where R gully (Jim's Gully) goes up steeply towards tree. Climb this and finish either in true continuation (Difficult) or ascend narrow chimney going up L. This route has many caves and chimneys and finishes in steep chockstone capped corner. Break out R at top.

59.b **Boomerang Gully**

850ft Winter, Difficult–Very Difficult (2 hours)*: FA *J Black, R G Donaldson, W H Murray January 1949*

Take easy snow slope into gully to pitch on R which leads to gully above (often iced). (It is easier to go straight on and reach top up face.)

58 Opposite: Stob Coire nan Lochan from the Gearr Aonach Ridge. On the left, above figure is the exit of McArtney's Gully. a,c= Access routes. b= Easy access route to summit up NW ridge, also a descent route from West Face of Aonach Dubh. 1=Easy face route. 2=Boomerang Gully left branch. 3=Boomerang Gully. 4=Broad Gully. 5=Dorsal Arete. 6,7=Forked Gully. 8=Twisting Gully. 9=South Centre Gully. 10=North Centre Gully. 11=North Face. 12=North Gully. 13=Pinnacle Gully (an easy snow climb)

59 Overleaf: Stob Coire nan Lochan (3657ft), Glencoe

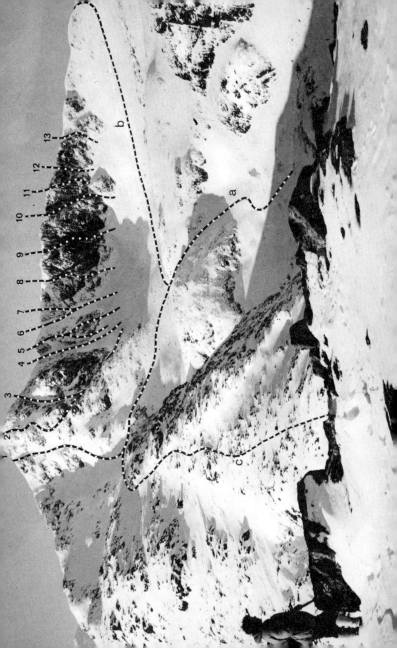

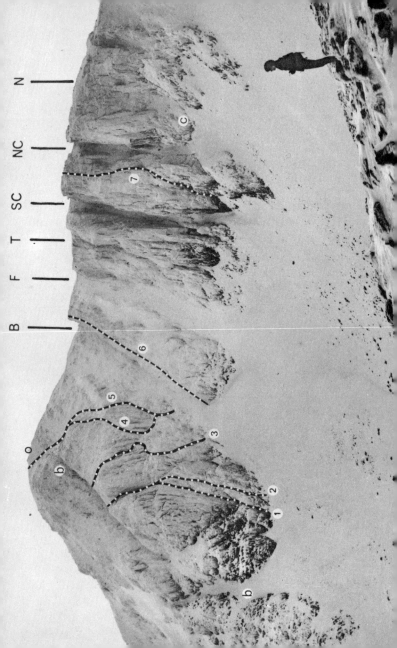

59.1 Scabbard Chimney

500ft Winter, Very Severe (5–8 hours)**: FA *L S Lovat, J R Marshall, A Hendry February 1956*

This route is seldom in good winter condition. Climb from close to lowest rocks of Summit Buttress up obvious chimney slanting up R. The crux, a sentry box, 200ft up, may need direct aid. A gully on the L above chimney leads to arete.

59.2 Spectre

400ft Winter, Very Severe (5–7 hours)**: FA *K Bryan, J Simpson January 1958*

This route runs parallel to Scabbard Chimney, and starts 40ft to R of that route. Up wall, 70ft to a point under first main chimney section of Scabbard Chimney. Go up R to gain snow ledge, follow this for 20ft, and down 8ft to long shelf. Up ice bulge above and groove to P B. Climb slab above, 25ft to bulge, continue 70ft to wide ledge. TR into the gully finish of Scabbard Chimney.

59.3 Innuendo

500ft Winter, Very Severe (3–4 hours)***: FA *H MacInnes, R Birch, P Judge, R O'Shea 1969*

Start level with bottom of Dorsal Arete. It takes an obvious chimney-groove for 120ft to ledge on L then goes on up into an overhung bay. Exit is by crack on R wall (crux) and easy snow is followed diagonally R to a block B below upper wall. TR R beneath a hanging chimney until steep cracks lead back L into chimney above overhang. The chimney is climbed direct, and easier slope to edge of Boomerang Gully.

59 4,5 Langsam

700ft Winter, Very Difficult (1 hour)*: FA *H MacInnes, M C MacInnes and party March 1969*

This route starts from Broad Gully and goes up snow slope to under rock wall. There are two routes from this point. First route: TR L on steep snow up then R to enter short gully and so to top bearing slightly R to summit. Alternatively take chimney under wall from top of first pitch under rock wall and climb this to top. Continue TR under wall and ascend steeper snow up L (crux), to gain easy snow line to summit.

59 **Pearly Gates**

500ft Very Difficult (1 hour)* : FA *I Clough and party April 1966*
This route leaves Broad Gully half way up on L (just under the
figure 5) and a narrow gap is visible on the skyline. Go up in
zig-zags to this point, 150ft and go through gap and follow to
top via Langsam line.

59.B **Broad Gully**

600ft
(Access route, Easy).

59.6 **Dorsal Arete**

300ft Winter, Difficult ($\frac{1}{2}$–1 hour)** : FA *J Black, T Shepherd,
J Allingham, J Bradburn 1951*
A rock arete situated between Broad and Forked Gullies. Access
from Broad Gully at base of arete. At top finish by slab to R or
by chimney (steep) on L (above narrow arete). Variation starts.

59.F **Forked Gully**

500ft Winter (1–2$\frac{1}{2}$ hours)*
Right Fork, Mild Severe; Left Fork, Moderate
The L fork gives an easy snow climb. The R (R of 200ft rock rib)
is steeper and holds ice.

59.T **Twisting Gully**

500ft Winter, Severe (2–3 hours)*** : FA *W H Murray, D Scott,
J C Simpson December 1946*
This gully is separated from Forked Gully by an indefinite rib;
to its R is South Buttress. The route takes the line of a shallow
gully. Go up 100ft into recess. From this point there are two
continuations. The original route takes chimney on L to bulge,
then TR L across gully wall to reach L rib. Mantelshelf move on
short arete, then easier above to final snow fan.

Right Fork

Winter, Severe (3 hours) : FA *J R Marshall, I D Haig January
1958*
This is a more difficult and direct line on the middle section of
original route. From recess, take steep ice pitch up corner. A
broken rib separates this from original route. The original route
is gained under final fan.

59.SC SC Gully

500ft Winter, Severe (3–5 hours)*** : FA *P D Baird, L Clinton, F Clinton March 1934*

This is the steep gully between Central and South Buttresses. There is usually an ice pitch low down, which can be turned on L. Go up on steep snow to point where R TR is made to gain a gangway (sometimes with bulge before top). P B often necessary. Steep and straightforward climbing to top.

59.7 Central Buttress

550ft Winter, Severe (2–3 hours)** : FA *H Raeburn, Dr Inglis Clark, Mrs Inglis Clark April 1907*

From a bay go up to R to gain crest. Up ridge to tower (turn on R) and regain crest by short chimney. Continue to top.

59.NC NC Gully

600ft Difficult ($\frac{3}{4}$–1 hour)**

Winter: The gully is between steep flanking walls. There can be an ice pitch short way up with B in cave on R.

59.N North Gully

250ft Winter, Difficult ($\frac{3}{4}$–1 hour)

This gully separates North Buttress from Pinnacle Buttress. Only the last section of gully is steep. Climb ice groove leading to R of cornice and turn the latter usually on R or tunnel (sometimes very large cornice). Exit just R of North Gully.

Right Chimney

250ft Severe ($\frac{3}{4}$–1 hour) : FA *H MacInnes February 1950*

Climb obvious ice chimney to R of North Gully, last pitch crux, climb up crack to L or easier to R.

59.C North Face

300ft Winter, Severe (2–3 hours) : FA *L S Lovat, K Bryan January 1956*

From under steep rock at bottom of North Buttress TR R to snow ledge. Ascend to recess high up on face. Up steep groove from L end of ledge to a nose and an arete.

60 Previous page: A big cornice in North Gully, Stob Coire nan Lochan

61 Opposite: The East Face of Aonach Dubh, Glencoe. 1 = Quiver Rib. 2 = Archer Ridge. 3 = Anonymous. 4 = Dangle. Circle marks climbers

61.5 **Drain Pipe Corner**

200ft grade —v**: FA *W Smith, C Vigano 1951*
Four interesting pitches on fine rock. First pitch, 50ft is crux
and the last pitch is also severe.

61.6 **Grochan Grooves**

160ft grade —v*: FA *J Cullen, C Vigano*
Climb shattered groove to tree, 65ft. Follow up wall trending
R, then L to grass ledge, tree. Up 20ft wall to R of tree to small
ledge. TR R to slab and recessed corner. Up corner to rowan
tree.

61.7 **Turnspit**

200ft grade —VI: FA *D Haston, R Smith 1961*
60ft L of Little Boomerang, climb wall to L of arete for 50ft
then TR R into crack and on to B. Go L up wall to finish.

61.8 **Little Boomerang**

220ft grade —v*: FA *M Noon, J Cunningham 1955*
From a point 20ft L of Boomerang, climb 15ft to base of crack,
passing small chockstone to where a long L step is made.
Straight up over bulge to easier ground, ST, B. Take crack above
for 115ft to ash tree, TR L 5ft to B. TR up R to bulging crack.
Climb this to top.

61.9 **Boomerang**

300ft grade v+**: FA *J Cunningham, M Noon 1955*
An obvious crack cleaves a big overhang. Climb wall next to
crack (use part of crack), to ST, B; 50ft. Up corner and crack to
overhanging nose (P runner high on R). Take long L step onto
shelves, B. Follow up crack to chockstone B at cave. Up crack
100ft to top.

61.10 **Original Route**

300ft grade —v: FA *C M Allan, J H B Bell 1934*
The climb takes the line of an obvious chimney. Up lower
chimney section towards big tree under main chimney. There
is a B 20ft above tree. Up steep chimney crack into wider
section above with chockstones and on to top.

62 East Face of Aonach Dubh, Glencoe. There are no good descent
routes down the North Face of Aonach Dubh from the top. Circles
mark climbers. 15=Drainpipe Corner. T=Terrace

122

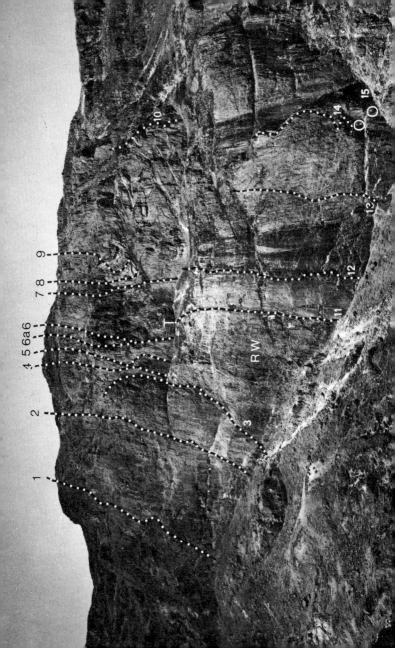

62.1 Barn Wall Route

500ft grade I: FA *D B McIntyre, T J Ransley, W H Murray 1947*
From highest point of the foot of the wall, climb by line of least resistance.

62.2 Bowstring

600ft grade III*: FA *D B McIntyre, W H Murray 1947*
Approx. 100ft up and L of the rowan tree and directly under a chimney on face, climb 8oft to slab under vertical wall. Move R across slab and up corner to grass ledge. Slant up L to the chimney. Up this, 2oft. Take either side of chimney to top.

62.3 Lower and Upper Bow

450ft grade IV* (grade II to Terrace): FA *J Neill, A H Henson 1946*
Ascend obvious shallow groove to Terrace: above, take the chimney line (unpleasant in wet).

62.RW Rowan-Tree Wall

250ft grade IV*: FA *W H Murray, D B McIntyre 1947*
Ascend any one of three cracks, 30ft R of obvious depression of Lower Bow. R crack is harder. 90ft up angle eases, scrambling easy to Terrace.

62.4 Quiver Rib

200ft grade III***: FA *D B McIntyre, W H Murray 1947*
Climb obvious rib just R of Upper Bow. A narrow groove trends L above, up steep face. Climb groove.

62.5 Arrow Wall

200ft grade IV**: FA *L S Lovat, J M Johnstone 1953*
Climb groove between Quiver Rib and Archer Ridge, slant R at 40ft. Continue on trend then directly up and make TR up L to broad ledge. TR L (Quiver Rib B). Up steep narrow black groove above (Quiver Rib groove leads up L), continue on groove to top.

62.6,6a **Archer Ridge**

250ft grade IV** : FA *W H Murray, D B McIntyre 1947*

Climb up crest of obvious ridge for 110ft to B below overhangs. TR R 20ft to B under wall. Up wall, 40ft to easier rock. Easy to big niche and B below short steep wall. Up on R part of wall to top.

Direct Finish grade IV** : FA *L S Lovat, I McNicol, A Way 1954*

Keep to crest of ridge (don't TR), and up bulge. Keep to ridge until big bulge is reached. TR L under this, then back R to steep crest to top.

62.7 **Basin Chimney**

250ft grade IV : FA *D Scott, J Currie Henderson 1947*

Direct to Basin by waterslides. From top L corner of Basin ascend to chimney (grassy gully to start with), then up loose rock and L to chimney. 90ft to top.

62.8 **G String**

250ft grade −V* : FA *W Smith, W Rowney 1955*

From the Basin, under obvious overhangs (route goes L of overhangs) TR up and L into groove; 35ft. Up groove to grass ledge, B; 70ft. Go round L into steep groove and up to grassy recess. Finish up crack at rear of recess.

62.9 **The Gut**

250ft grade VI : FA *J Cunningham, W Smith 1956*

From under the jagged overhangs of the Basin go to slabby scoop, 10ft to R of trees. Up scoop past overlap, 15ft and bulge (loose rock); 40ft. Diagonally L to grass ledge to B (also used for G String); 90ft. The following pitch of 120ft is the crux. Ascend wall above, 15ft, TR R horizontally to big groove below one of the large overhangs. Ascend groove, 15ft, gain ledge on R, TR R for a few ft, and up steep wall to B at top.

62.10 **Terrace Arete**

100ft grade −V* : FA *P Walsh, J Cullen*

Start at cairn below small arete. Climb 15ft up awkward step to gain arete. Up to large ledge; 50ft. On up L edge; 35ft.

62.11 **Anonymous**

200ft grade IV* : FA *Unknown*

From just above Spider take a direct line up wall to Terrace.

62.12 **Spider**

200ft grade V+* : FA *J R Marshall, A H Hendry 1957*

To the L of the waterslide bands and below the rowan tree go up wall 20ft to obvious grass ledge. Follow up wall 30ft, TR R into groove on L edge of waterslide. Up groove, 20ft, TR L to thin crack. Ascend crack (P runner), to ledge. Up wall to broad ledge; 100ft. Easier for 80ft to Terrace.

62.13 **The Long Crack**

300ft grade −V* : FA *L S Lovat, J M Johnstone 1953*

An obvious feature on Weeping Wall is a long crack trending R 10ft then directly up almost to Terrace; it starts about centre of wall, R of waterslide bands. The route gains crack directly from below and follows it to Terrace. At detached block at base of wall, near R end go up 15ft to horizontal ledge. TR R to steep groove. Up groove and steep wall above, directly to base of crack, 80ft, P B. Climb wall just R of crack (crux), gain grass ST on groove. Follow in crack to Terrace.

62.14 **Dangle By-Pass**

220ft grade IV** : FA *H MacInnes, M C MacInnes 1965*

This route starts from the small shelf to L of Drainpipe Corner. Route goes up L of overhang and back up R to B. TR up R onto edge and up to top.

63 Overleaf left: Archer Ridge, East Face of Gearr Aonach, Glencoe

64 Overleaf right: Dangle, East Face of Aonach Dubh, Glencoe. A pleasant problem for a damp day

65 Opposite: The North Face of Aonach Dubh, Glencoe. The slanting dotted line below Ossian's Cave (O) is the Sloping Shelf. This can be gained from the bridge just East of Coire nan Lochan stream (across the River Coe), or from the west and south sides of Loch Achtriochtan, or by fording the river across from Achtriochtan Farm. Pleasant Terrace in summer is a Grade I route. Descent from the summit in winter should be via the Stob Coire nan Lochan basin

Soft grade AI: *Dangle Overhang* FA *I Clough and another 1965*
This is a pleasant artificial route for a wet day. It goes up R
from the shelf mentioned onto steep wall, trending R then up
overhang to finish at the B of the By-Pass.

65.1 Waterfall Wall

400ft grade −V**: FA *D Goldie, R Goldie 1955*
Route goes up L wall of gully. From access route go up first
short pitch of gully. Ascend wall from cairn slanting slightly L,
30ft (awkward move L at P runner), B at 8oft. Up to big block;
6oft. TR 30ft R on rock shelf, up 4oft to sloping ledge (P B). Up
short wall to R and on to close to top of buttress by long (IV)
runout. 4oft to top.

65.2 Shadbolt's Chimney

550ft Winter, Very Severe (7–9 hours)**: FA (Winter) *D Goldie,
R Goldie February 1955*
This climb is to L of Ossian's Cave. Go up deep chimney from
the Sloping Shelf for 150ft. Up buttress on R, or up to 30ft
chimney which leads to the amphitheatre. A wide snow gully
leads to top. This route is seldom in true winter conditions.

65.0 Ossian's Ladder

200ft grade II: FA *Neil Marquis (Shepherd) 1868*
This is the route into Ossian's Cave. From Sloping Shelf directly
below Cave, climb up to cave floor (this slopes at 45°).

65.3P Pleasant Terrace

8ooft Winter, Hard Severe (3–4 hours)**: FA *J McArtney,
I Clough January 1969*
Start from the upper R end of Sloping Shelf. Start from bay to
L of Deep Gash Gully. Go up L in two pitches. The second can
be hard, and starts as a corner crack. The Terrace narrows to a
spectacular ledge going horizontally L for several hundred ft.
The ledge broadens after a slight descent, under a deep narrow
chimney; this is taken to the top.

65.4 **Yo-Yo**

300ft grade VI+**: FA *R Smith, D Hughes 1959*

The climb takes the prominent corner midway between Deep Gash Gully and Ossian's Cave. Go up and L for 20ft from an undercut flake to a slab, then up R into corner. There is P B 110ft up on ledge on L. Up corner to B above main overhang; 70ft. Follow on 100ft with short deviation to L near top.

Yo-Yo (Continuation above Pleasant Terrace)

200ft grade VI+: FA *J Moriarty, R Smith 1960*

Follow up the continuation by a grooved arete and short overhanging corner to top.

65.5 **Deep Gash Gully**

200ft Winter, Very Severe (4–7 hours)**: FA *J Cunningham, M Noon February 1957*

This is the obvious gully just above end of the Shelf. Though the climb is short it is technically hard. There is a 30ft chimney pitch, a steep ice pitch leading to the main overhang. A thread B in a hole in the roof is used and up rope using slings to gain B. The final pitch, 40ft, entails going through a small hole feet first. An ice overhang is climbed above. Steep snow to top.

66.d **Dinner-Time Buttress**

600ft Winter (1–2 hours)

This buttress provides a means of access to Stob Coire nan Lochan. The usual route is to turn into Gully 2 at the start of the upper rock (above the steep waterfall pitches in the gully) and ascend gully. The Buttress itself can provide a pleasant climb in icy conditions (Difficult–Very Difficult). The TR to Middle Ledge can be awkward in winter and a difficult sloping shelf is followed (frequently iced) up and round corner to R from the start of the easy upper section of Gully 2. Another approach is via lower section of B Buttress. Gully 1 is of little interest and is rather indefinite. Gully 2 offers a good descent route, though steep, and shouldn't be glissaded.

66 *Overleaf:* The West Face of Aonach Dubh showing the approach from just west of main road bridge at the cross roads. The gullies and buttresses are described in the text with the exception of Gully 4 and Buttress F. For winter, a further descent route runs right across top of face on easy slopes down into the Bidean corrie

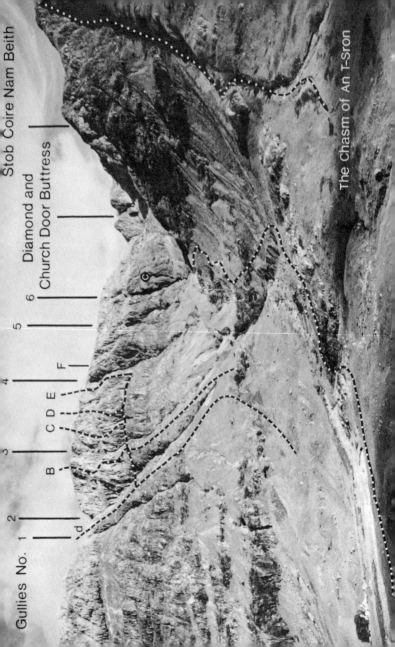

Gullies No. 1   2   3   4   5   6

Stob Coire Nam Beith

Diamond and
Church Door Buttress

d   B   C D E   F

The Chasm of An T-Sron

66. B B Buttress, The Pinnacle Face
300ft grade III : FA *J H B Bell, C M Allan 1932*
Climb up B Buttress to Middle Ledge. From just below Middle
Ledge, three pinnacles can be seen above. To the L of pinnacles
a groove runs down. Up a chimney, under L pinnacle and R of
groove towards R pinnacle (good rock).

66.3 Gully 3
1000ft Winter, Severe (4–5 hours)* : FA *Crofton, Evans March
1934*
The Gully is shallow and somewhat indefinite. It is better
defined where it cuts the Middle Tier.

66. C C Buttress
500ft Winter, Very Difficult (2 hours)* : FA *A Taylor, A Thomp-
son, K Whithall, A Smith, J McArtney February 1969*
Go across from Middle Ledge or up lower part of B Buttress.
Climb up a short wide chimney on the R and take the obvious
crest.

66 The Screen
200ft Winter, Very Severe (3–5 hours)*** : FA *D Bathgate,
J Brumfitt February 1965*
This is the prominent icefall which forms on the lower tier to
R of Gully 3. It forms a direct start to C-D Scoop which is
between C and D Buttresses on Middle Tier. By TR R ascend
70ft to icicle recess, TR R and back L above to final ice runnel.

66 C-D Scoop
500ft Winter, Very Difficult (1½ hours from start to Rake)** :
FA *D Bathgate, J Brumfitt February 1965*
This route can be reached from Gully 2 and is the second gully
on L. The route gives two short pitches. Exit along The Rake,
or continue by the hidden branch of a gully to L, the continuation of Gully 3 above The Rake. The route makes a good
continuation to The Screen.

66. D D Buttress
500ft Winter, Severe (2–3 hours)* : FA *P Mallinson, D Power,
J Choat, J Friend, I Clough February 1969*
Up steep prominent icy gangway just R of C-D Scoop. Above,

go R, L and R on zig-zagging ramps and ledges, to crest and take short steep grooved wall. Easier above.

67.B Gully 5 (Left Start)

1000ft Winter, Severe (3–5 hours): FA *A Fyffe, N Clough, C MacInnes*

To avoid lower overhanging ice pitch, start further to L at a subsidiary gully. Start up chimney to reach small cave. Move up and R over ice fall to reach crest of small buttress. Climb buttress to below Needle's Eye (approx. line of Original Route). Move R into gully proper and continue up gully over one small ice pitch at the bottom, taking L fork at point where gully is split by rib at above half height.

66.6 Gully 6

800ft Winter, Very Severe (4–6 hours)***: FA *D H Munro, P D Smith March 1951*

This gully usually gives a continuous ice climb in good conditions. Several fine pitches.

66.c Chaos Chimney

500ft Winter, Hard Severe (2 hours): FA *A Fyffe and party*

This is the chimney/gully to R of Gully 6. Start at base of chimney at bottom of 6 and climb two small ice pitches to where chimney deepens and narrows. Up large ice pitch on L and then on R. Continue over two further ice pitches to top.

67 The Chasm of An T-Sron

1200ft Winter, Severe (4–5 hours): FA *Not recorded 1959 or 1960?*

This chasm splits the north face, and starts at about 1000ft. Five pitches but most of the gully is easy. Three of the pitches are waterfalls and can give good ice pitches. The first, a large one, is avoided on the L flank. Seldom in true winter conditions.

67 The West Face of Aonach Dubh. A=Middle Ledge. B=Gully 5 Left Start. 5=Gully 5. 2=The Big Top. 3=Trapeze. 4=Hee-Haw. Photograph is taken from Bidean path above the waterfall. a=The Amphitheatre in Gully 4

67.1 Consolation

270ft grade v* : FA *G Grandison, I Clough 1962*

Climb heathery groove approx. on nose of buttress (a big spike indicates start), to reach some B under twin cracks. Gain R crack and up to recess under overhang. Go L round rib to B at base of small chimney. Up then L, 40ft to B. 100ft of slabs and scrambling to top.

68.1 The Big Top

520ft grade vi*** : FA *R Smith, J Gardener 1961*

Reach routes 1, 2 and 3 via Middle Ledge from Dinner-Time Buttress. Start from block B under arete. Pitch 1 ; Up and L 50ft, ascend slabby corner, then up and R to B on big flake; 110ft. Pitch 2 ; Up arete on R then a bulge above and follow by crack on arete edge to easier angled rock; 110ft. (Slabs run L from here to easy buttress crest.) Pitch 3 ; Go R into slanting line of slabby grooves. Up these until feasible to go L into 10ft crack. Up this to big ledge, B; 150ft. Pitch 4 ; Up big flake on R to gain wall, go L up wall then R and TR R across groove to slab. P in place. Up slab and wall and end up broken groove to top; 150ft.

68.2 Trapeze

450ft grade vi*** : FA *J R Marshall, D Leaver 1958*

Start near the L edge of the sw face of E Buttress at rakes, which run to base of obvious corner, B. Up corner (strenuous) past ST (P runner) at 20ft, B under overhang; 70ft. Turn overhang on L and up corner (easy) to slabs running to mossy bay; 140ft. TR R 20ft to obvious platform. The following pitch is 130ft. Leave platform on L and up steep wall to ledge and corner above. The corner is turned on the R then a rising R TR to groove and crack. Up these to slab, under an overhang, TR R to bay, B. Take a groove R and a short crack to top.

68.3 Hee-Haw

400ft grade —vi*** : FA *J Moriarty, D Haston 1959*

This route is reached up Gully 4 from Middle Ledge. Up steep groove on edge of small buttress to grass ledge; 80ft. Up corner

68 The South West Face of E Buttress, Aonach Dubh, Glencoe, looking across from F Buttress. In the foreground is Gully 4. ML= Middle Ledge. In the background is the Aonach Eagach Ridge. Circles indicate climbers

crack, 20ft and steep wall, 100ft to detached block under obvious crack, P B. Up this overhanging crack, P runner to under big overhang. Up R on steep wall to ledge, P B. TR L into groove (steep), follow to end. Go L 90ft to small ST on slab. Up slab, finish by crack (overhanging) close to buttress top.
Note. The best descent route is across the wide ledge (The Rake) from the top of the Buttress to Gully 2, down this then onto Dinner-Time Buttress a short way above Middle Ledge.

72.1,2 Broken Gully

500ft Very Difficult (1½–2 hours): FA *I Clough, Mrs Clough January 1966*
Ascend L into recess above wide snow shelf which cuts Buttress 1 into two tiers. 100ft up, a shallow gully on R is taken to easy L TR out to top of buttress. The L fork is harder (very difficult–severe) and holds more ice.

72.3 Buttress 1

700ft Winter, Severe (2–3 hours): FA *I Clough and party March 1967*
Up chimney line in a series of ice pitches. Above chimney TR easily L to reach top of buttress, or continue to summit. Grade 1 (Summer).

72.4 Arch Gully

600ft Winter, Severe (1½–3 hours)*: FA (Direct Route) *unknown*
This Gully is between Buttresses 1 and 2. It is a poor summer route. The lower section is usually banked over, but can give a

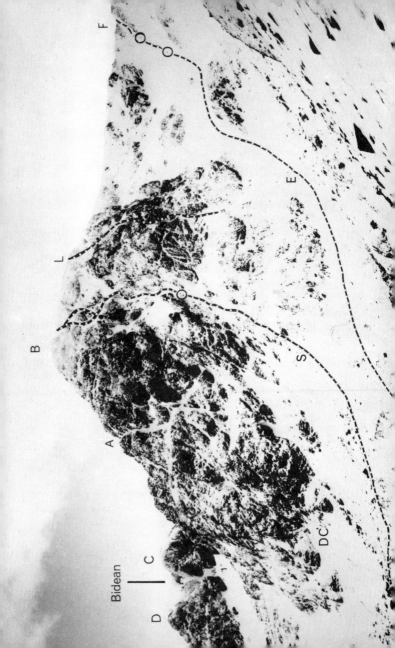

few pitches. A narrowing slope leads to two steep ice pitches, which can be climbed direct, or turned without much trouble. Easy slopes to top (400ft).

72.5 **Central Gully**

1500ft Winter, Severe–Very Severe (3–5 hours)** : FA *J Clarkson, J Waddell January 1958*
This gully starts above and just L of the lowest rocks of Buttress 3. It holds a lot of ice and gives a fine route.

72.DC **Deep Cut Chimney**

1500ft Winter, Severe (3–6 hours)*** : FA *W M MacKenzie, W H Murray April 1939*
This climb offers several short ice pitches, the longest usually 40ft. After approx. 400ft the Chimney reaches a small amphitheatre where it is easy to continue to the R to crest of Buttress 4, close to fork of North West Gully. From the amphitheatre, the L fork can be hard if covered with verglas. This line goes L taking long steep crack line to easier ground above.

72.6 **North West Gully**

1500ft Very Difficult (2–4 hours)** : FA *Glover, Worsdell April 1906*
Variation possible on this route: start as shown on illustration or TR in from R from bottom of the Pyramid. Easy up to L of Sphinx Buttress; above gully has two forks. The L one is straightforward (A). The R fork goes up L of upper section of the Sphinx, several hundred feet to further fork. The L fork can have an ice pitch leading to shoulder (steep wall to L of shoulder can be quite hard sometimes). Easy to top from shoulder.

72.7 **Smashed Spectacles Gully**

500ft Severe (1½–2 hours)* : FA *I Clough, F Jones, R Fox, C Wood February 1969*
This is the R of two diverging couloirs. There is a short ice pitch in first part, followed by a very steep chimney with ice bulge above. Above, easier to top.

72 Stob Coire nam Beith. The route to Bidean goes up under this face. R=descent route from col

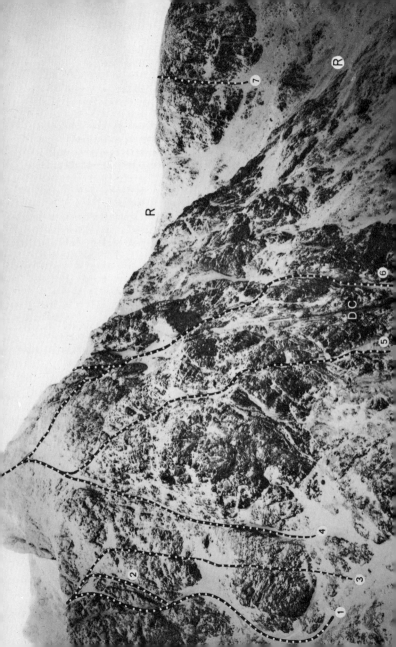

73.2 **Left Wall**

1000ft grade IV* : FA *R L Plackett, R Bumstead 1939*
Take line of least resistance up section of triangular rock
between Buttresses 2 and 3.

73.4 **The Mummy**

200ft grade IV** : FA *I Clough, C Kynaston, J Garster 1966*
Take a central line up this small buttress, easily gained by L TR
from below final wall of the Sphinx. Up first groove, until
possible to go L to ledge, B. Follow cracks and grooves to top.

73.5 **The Sphinx**

450ft grade III** : FA *W H Murray, R Smith 1946*
Access is from NW Gully. Midway on N face is a black cave.
Go L under and just L of cave by shattered wall. Up to small
basin below cave. TR R to ledge under vertical upper rocks. Up
walls to chimney, enter small recess 10ft up R. Use pinnacle-
flake, go R and up. 250ft to top.

73.6 **The Pyramid**

300ft grade III : FA *W H Murray 1946*
There are two buttresses, one above the other to w of NW
Gully. The lower one is the Pyramid. Go up N ridge, with
mantelshelf at 140ft. There is an exposed wall higher, near L edge.
Winter Very Difficult (2–4 hours)** : FA *J R Marshall,
I Douglas Janaury 1958*

73.7 **Isis**

200ft grade V+ : FA *I Clough, M Large, M Hadley 1959*
Close to bottom rocks of clean wall ascend between open
inclined gully at base of prominent groove with a pedestal 10ft
up R wall. Up groove to ledge (grassy), and some B; 8oft (P
runner used). Up overhanging flake crack above, or L across
slabs, up steep wall and take gangway back R to above flake.
Continue to top (easier).

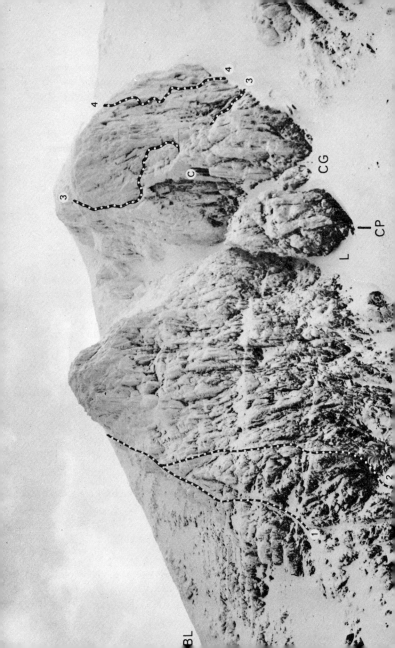

74.L **Adagio**

500ft Winter, Very Severe (3 hours) : FA *H MacInnes, D Chen, R Birch, P Judge, R O'Shea 1969*

This climb is on w side of buttress to R of Summit Gully. It takes line of a steep narrow gully. Easy snow leads to a steeper section with thinly iced wall on L. This is passed by climbing a corner on R and making a difficult L rising TR round corner to gain other ice chimney. This L chimney is climbed for 20ft before moving into R-hand one above bulge. Go up R chimney 50ft. This leads to easier ground. The continuation follows main gully (keeping L) to big cave which is climbed direct. Gully now leads out onto top of buttress. Continue easily by ridge of Summit Gully or use Summit Gully as descent route. Note. Belays inadequate.

74.HG **Hidden Gully**

500ft Winter, Severe (2–4 hours)** : FA *L Lovat, W J R Greaves February 1955*

Climb to cave and up on L wall. Easy to further cave, passed on L by short ice pitch. Ahead is a saddle above a rib in centre of gully. The gully narrows and steepens above and a short chimney is climbed. There are two narrow exits above; take the L. It is steeper at top. Finish up Adagio or go R to Bootneck Gully.

74.B **Bootneck Gully**

800ft Winter, Severe (2 hours) : FA *H MacInnes, I Duckworth, P Wells, R Ward, J Parsons March 1969*

This route takes a central line up w face of Stob Coire nam Beith. It takes central chimney line which has a steep rock wall on its R with a possibly easier gangway start close under this. (The next chimney L leads to the top of a small rock buttress and goes up near Hidden Gully, severe.) After two pitches in gully/chimney a steep ice wall on R is climbed direct (crux). This leads onto long easy snow slopes which lead to summit of mountain, bearing R at fork.

---

75 *Previous page right:* Bidean nam Bian (3766ft). BL=Route down ridge to Bealach between Bidean and Stob Coire nan Lochan. L=Left branch of Central Gully. CP=Collie's Pinnacle. C=Crypt Route to left and Flake Route to right. 4=Kingpin ; summer route only

75.1 **North Route**

700ft Winter, Severe (2–4 hours)* : FA *J Clarkson; F King February 1955*

This route takes the L edge of the buttress by scoops and chimneys to rock arete. (Escape to L possible.)

75.2 **North Route Variation**

220ft to N Route Winter, Severe (3–4 hours)* : FA *L S Lovat, W Harrison March 1955*

This climb takes an obvious scoop to R of North Route. The scoop is steep and finally overhangs. Climb arete to the R and make short horizontal TR round corner into further scoop. Snow-covered slabs and crack (crux) lead to ledge above the overhang of initial scoop. TR L to crest of North Route.

75.CG **Central Gully**

450ft Winter, Moderate**

This Gully is between Church Door and Diamond Buttresses. The bottom of the gully is divided by Collie's Pinnacle. The main branch (R) is straightforward and continues directly to top. There is a further branch to the L near top and yet another to the R. The top R is harder. The bottom fork to L of Collie's Pinnacle can be very difficult in winter, or harder.

75.3 **West Chimney**

700ft Winter, Very Severe (3–6 hours)*** : FA *A Fyffe, H Mac-Innes (through leads) February 1969*

Ascend L slanting chimney to under, then up, large chockstones to B under overhang; 150ft. Up short steep wall to gain cave and through-route to roof. Go R from exit chimney to Flake Route Arch and B. Continue across gap to B under steep crack above Crypt Route (exposed). Up crack, B at top. Follow up, slanting L, then up icy slab to summit slopes. The section from Flake Route up is also used for Crypt Route. (P B used and two for runners.)

75.4 **Kingpin**

350ft grade VI+** : FA *J Hardie, W Thomson (through leads) 1968*

Near middle of face and starting 150ft up is a long nose with a corner either side. The route takes an almost direct line to the L corner. 1. 6oft (VI) Start at short crack (arrow and cairn), climb to slab. TR 1oft to corner below smooth groove, up corner

(1 P) moving R into groove. B at top of groove. 2. 6oft (VI) Take ramp on R then mantelshelf onto ledge below chimney cutting roof. Up chimney (1 P) and out L to small B. 3. 110ft (VI) Back to top of chimney, climb gangway on R (2 P if wet) to small hooded recess. Up and out R to edge. Follow grooves trending R to foot of big corner. 4. 8oft (VI) Climb crack to roof. Move R (1 P) to small ledge on face of nose. Up wall to ledge at top of corner. 5. 4oft (3+) Climb chimney groove to top.

77.a Crack Line

26oft grade VI** : FA *J Hardie, W Thomson 1968*
Start at groove with twin cracks, 25ft L of Crypt Route (arrow). Up groove to ledge on R and follow by cracks to P B, 4oft under arch; 110 ft. Up line of groove trending to L end of arch, 5oft up, go L into steep groove. Follow this to the end and go L onto moss covered slab running to corner, B; 110ft. Up cracks on R corner wall (arrow) to B at top of Raeburn's Chimney; 4oft. Finish up Crypt Route.

77.b Crypt Route

18oft grade IV*** : FA *Morley Wood, Wilding, A Pigott 1920*
Go up chimney, 7oft to rock passage which goes into buttress. From back of passage (dark) are various routes: *The Tunnel Route* Through narrow passage in L wall, into rock chamber (total darkness). A further tunnel goes to second chamber; from this a long narrow tunnel goes up to aperture in face of cliff, 2oft below R side of arch. Up 2oft to hole in lower R end of arch. Continue by ordinary Flake Route. *The Through Route* Ascend cave-like end of passage to second smaller cave. Direct exit is overhanging and spectacular.

The Gallery Variation: FA *I G Norris, P Barker 1952*
Grade IV, 18oft. Take through route to second cave, ascend into another chimney in same fault going to third cave (smaller). Go into the Gallery above, 6 × 20 × 4ft high. Go down 4ft from Gallery floor and facing outwards, TR 5oft R and climb up to base of arch.

76 Opposite: The three exit routes from Central Gully Bidean nam Bian. The right one is the hardest, Very Difficult

77 Overleaf: Church Door Buttress, Bidean nam Bian. A climber can be seen in Crypt Route (b). This photograph was taken from Central Gully

Winter Hard Severe (3–5 hours)*** : FA *H MacInnes and party February 1960*
The Tunnel Route was taken on the first ascent and had little ice. In heavy ice conditions the route could be harder.

77.f Flake Route
350ft grade IV** : FA *H Raeburn, J H Bell, H Boyd, R Napier 1898*
Up crack to top of Buttress, above flake, make awkward step R round corner. Straight up (II) until L TR can be done to arch of Church Door. Cross arch to a 30ft chimney (crux). Face R wall. Above chimney up steep face to easy ground under cairn, or avoid face by harder chimney on its L.

Winter Hard Severe (3–4 hours)** : FA *H MacInnes and party February 1960*
The summer route was followed throughout. In hard ice conditions the climb could be Very Severe.

80.A Hourglass Gully
400ft Difficult***
This gully is straightforward, but sometimes has two short sections.

80.C The Gash
400ft Severe–Very Severe (2–3 hours)*** : FA *I Clough, M Hadley, M Large March 1959*
Reach gully by rising TR L from bottom of Hourglass Gully, or ascend direct, ST on R. Directly up steep ice and bulges above. Climb overhanging chockstone on L to cave under second big chockstone slab. Up through-route at back of cave to narrow exit.

Gash right fork: Winter, Very Difficult (20 minutes) : FA *H MacInnes, A N Other February 1971*

Sgor na h-Ulaidh 3258ft
Access to this peak is up a side road opposite Achnacon Farm at the W end of Glencoe. Walk up this road, round farm and keep to the L fork of the Allt na Muide to Sgor na h-Ulaidh

78 *Overleaf left:* Bidean nam Bian. The step across the 'gap' on Church Door Buttress in winter

79 *Overleaf right:* Bidean nam Bian. Traverse across the arch on Church Door Buttress to the steep crack in winter

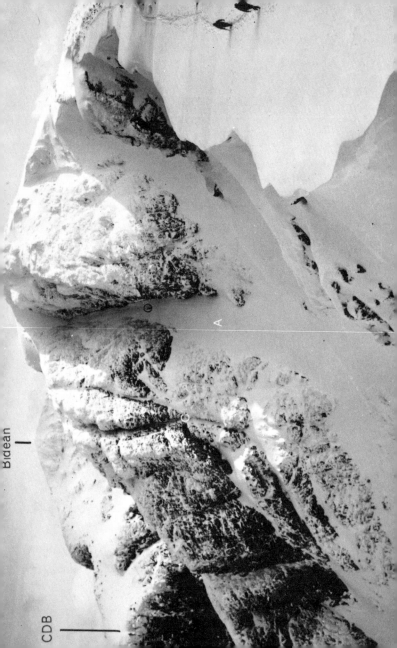

ahead and to the L. Vixen Gully can be used for descent when there is sufficient snow to blank-out the small pitches or the descent as shown on the photograph leading onto the easy ridge of Aonach Dubh a'Chinne (R).

81.1 Subsidiary Scoop
500ft Winter, Very Difficult* : FA *I Clough, Mrs Clough March 1966*
Just L of Red Gully on other side of rocky rib a line up steep snow is taken with short ice steps.

81.2 Red Gully
650ft Winter, Very Difficult (1½–4 hours)** : FA *D Scott, R Anderson, G Allison, G Black March 1948*
Climb gully direct which often has considerable ice late in the season. Some years the gully can be harder.

81.3 Brush Buttress
900ft Winter, Very Difficult (2 hours)* : FA *H MacInnes and party March 1969*
This buttress is in three tiers, the middle one being the hardest. Start from lowest rocks and climb direct. Start main buttress in central gully and move to edge on L. Gain ledge and B above; 80ft. Start in chimney above and climb this and B on L; 60ft. Continue up chimney line and TR R on narrow ledge. Finish on final buttress to L of steep edge, or up last section of main gully.

81.4 Vixen Gully
500ft Winter, Easy
An easy route to the summit, can sometimes be used for descent.

81.5 West Gully
1000ft Winter, Difficult (1½–3 hours) : FA *J G Parish, D H Haworth, J S Berkeley February 1948*
A straight snow climb, sometimes a bit awkward at top.

80 Previous page left: On the ridge between Bidean and Stob Coire nam Beith. CDB = Church Door Buttress. A climber can be seen in Hourglass Gully (A)

81 Previous page right: Sgor na h'Ulaidh, Glencoe. A view of the main face from the approach beyond Ghleann-leac-na-muidhe farm

Etive Slabs, Beinn Trilleachan

82.1 Claw

840ft grade —VI*: FA *M Noon, A Charles, T Lawrie 1957*
Start straight below dark streak marks under tree (cairn). Up
slab to grass, go R then L cross slab to ledge, up thin crack, TR L
passing dark streak and on up to grass ledge. Go R to rowan,
40ft L of Hammer; 150ft. Go directly up to grass ledge; 100ft.
Go across slab above tree in groove, up groove a short way; 50ft.
Take groove to top, TR R, pass spike runner to arete and on to
ledge; 120ft. Up then R round corner (awkward) and on to
short groove. Up this and flaw to slab and big block; 120ft. Go
up two short overhangs then slab above; 120ft. Up overhanging
chimney (P move up to ledge), thread runner, up smooth
walls and across to recess, tree B; 80ft. At top of recess, up crack
to R of twin cracks, complete route up slabs to B high up
(Eyehole B); 100ft.

82.7 The Long Walk

1400ft grade —VI: FA *J Cunningham, M Noon 1958*
Start at R of slabs. Go diagonally L up to ST under obvious
corner in first overlap (2 pitches; 250ft). Ascend corner crack,
sling used on spike. The crack widens (2 wedges) ST on slabs
above; 70ft. Slant L to B on next overlap edge (2 pitches; 250ft).
TR below overlap, using wedge runner, to Long Wait B (not
described); 80ft. Go L to ST under black wall; 80ft. Ascend wall
using sling on spike, to slabs above. Up slabs to tree B; 50ft.
Go L along zig-zag line of next overlap to ST (common to
Agony); 150ft. Continue up Agony to finish; 500ft.

83.1 Hammer

500ft grade V**: FA *M Noon, J Cunningham 1957*
Begin 30ft L of Agony at corner under tree. Up corner, tree B;
50ft. Follow steep grass to ledge; 120ft. Up shallow scoop
trending to L, into groove; on up groove P B. Up groove further
8ft to P; tension — TR R to small ledge. Up crack above to
overhang, move R, up short chimney and cross slab to good B
in corner. Descend short way then move across and up slab to
grass; 50ft.

82 *Overleaf:* Beinn Trilleachan Slabs, Glen Etive. m = Moustache. C =
Crevasse. 2 = Hammer. 3 = Frustration. 4 = Swastika. 5 = Pause.
6 = Spartan Slab

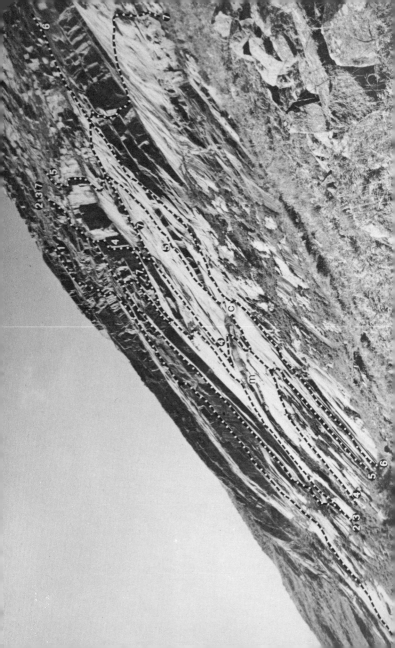

83.2 Agony

540ft grade — VI A1* : FA *J Cunningham, W Smith, M Noon 1957*
Begin at bottom of first obvious groove sweeping up the slabs;
to L of Spartan Slab. Up groove direct, using some P for direct
aid (8 used) to grassy patches; 120ft. Ascend these to grassy
ledge; flake B; 120ft. Follow up groove (16 P). Grassy ledge with
small ash tree at 110ft. P B in groove. Up groove (occasional
direct aid); 150ft to grassy patch in corner; 80ft, TR diagonally
R up slab to overhang under second grassy patch; ascend to top
of grass and go awkwardly, diagonally L to small rock shelf;
P B; 40ft. Up directly to overhang; tension – TR 15ft R to
reasonable holds, ST and P B. Ascend straight up corner above,
to small overhang; 80ft. Mantelshelf on this, up slab above to
overhanging wall, then TR L across awkward slab to ash B.
Directly up overhanging wall behind B; up slab above to flake
B; 30ft. Finish.

83.3 Frustration

600ft grade V+ : FA *D Haston, A Wightman 1960*
Begin on slab to R of Agony. Ascend crack, tension-TR (from P
at top) into parallel crack on R; up crack to B; 100ft. TR R until
ledge finishes; 30ft. Abseil from ledge to holds on edge of lower
overhang; go to R, then climb slabs to B; 70ft. Up corner on L
to ST under overlap; 150ft. Over overlap and slabs above to
meet Agony; P runner; 100ft. Directly up through overlap to
tree B; 100ft. L round corner and climb overlap to easy grass;
50ft.

83.4 Swastika

685ft grade — VI** : FA *M Noon, E Taylor*
Start 30ft beyond tree to L of Spartan Slab. Up slab on thin
crack to ledge (two P); 120ft. Go R across ledges to P B below
big block; 8oft. Ascend slab to block, surmount direct and go
to B under overhang; 40ft. Slightly R, tension-TR and put in
another above lip of overhang (now done free), mantelshelf
on overhang, TR L along the Moustache (narrow grass crack
along lip overhang) to grassy ledges; 90ft. Ascend quartz
band, slanting slightly R to grass and ledge; 115ft.

83 Overleaf left: The Glen Etive Slabs, Beinn Trilleachan. These are to
the west, up from the end of the Glen Etive Road. m=Moustache,
C=Crevasse

Follow up slab to ledge; 20ft. Follow quartz band to grassy patch under second line of overhangs; 8oft. TR 6ft L by P to overhanging corner; up by spike and a P; 6oft. Up slab above to tree B under big corner. Seven P used up smaller crack, L of main corner, to ledge under clean-cut overhang; 4oft. Go up and R to ledge in main corner. Follow up corner to another ledge; end by layback; 2oft.

83.5 The Pause

67oft grade —VI***: FA *J R Marshall, G J Ritchie, G Tiso, R Marshall 1960*

From prominent groove L of Spartan Slab, climb slab on its R. Move into groove at 6oft (three P runners only), follow groove, 25ft and exit by large spikehold to reach grass patch and P B. Up layback crack on lip of groove, then easy rocks to B of Swastika; 5oft. Climb Swastika to small overlap, TR by its R edge to under main overlap, and using small tree, TR into the Crevasse; 13oft. Reach slab above, go L into groove and up ledge on the slab 3oft (P runner); TR R to faint line of cracks, follow cracks to small overlap and go R to reach ST and P B; 13oft. Up R to the extreme R end of a higher overlap P runner then up thin crack to easy groove, this leads to large grass patch; 12oft. P B. Ascend overlaps on L to the bottom of terminal slab, TR L to an undercut edge which is ascended to gain a higher grass ledge; 1o0ft. End by vertical corner on L; 5oft.

83 The Long Reach

67oft grade VI+***: FA *J McLean, W Smith (through leads) 1963*

Climb middle of slab, 3oft R of Pause (arrow). Up to overlap, cross to B on L (Spartan's); 15oft. Up twin grooves above, onto slab, then horizontally L on small band, 15ft and slant L up line of small grooves to B below first big overlap; 14oft. Cross overlap via Swastika. Go R to B (junction with The Pause); 7oft. Crux, ascend slab via niche (P. runner) to overlap. PB 100 ft. TR L 1oft then directly up, past grassy pocket to small groove on R running to B under small overlap; 6oft. Continue straight up to below next big overlap. Go R and B under overhanging groove (arrow); 3oft. Surmount this using one P and groove above to ledge going L to sentry box. Up R up thin crack to grass ledge, B; 13oft. Up small corner above; 4oft.

84 Previous page right: First pitch, The Long Reach, Etive Slabs

85 Opposite: Etive Slabs. The tension traverse on Frustration

83.6 **Spartan Slab**

575ft grade v**: FA *E D G Langmuir, M J O'Hara, J A Mallinson 1954*

Begin 10ft L of big flat-topped block at base of the Great Slab. Up groove (some grass) 80ft, go R to lower slab and gain big ledge, 120ft, P B. Descend short way, step out R onto steep slab; layback thin flake until obvious overhanging flake at top of slab is reached. Go R into easy groove and up to niche, B under bowshaped overhang; 80ft. Move out L up into overhung niche, up overhang, B from crack above; 20ft. Straight up crack to reach horizontal crack, hand TR, 25ft and up to turf ledge and B; 50ft. Down and out onto slab on R, TR R, descend to niche, exit by R side until a move up and L to steep slab is feasible, 10 ft up narrow crack, step down R and across and up block to gain crack, climb this till it branches, follow cracks to P B and ST; 125ft. Up slab above, still slanting R; at top, TR to easier rock. Up 50ft cracked slab to vegetation under overhanging wall, B; 100ft. Twenty ft R of cairn is overhanging corner, climb a few ft, TR R to obvious nose followed by move to cave; up short chimney on L to easy ground.

Garbh Bheinn of Ardgour, General

Garbh Bheinn in the district of Ardgour lies west of Loch Linnhe and it is one of the most pleasant climbing areas in Scotland. The rock consists of a mixture of quartzite and quartzose-felspathic-gneiss with a predomination of gneiss. The rock is rough and sound with adequate small holds on what appear to be smooth slabs.

The peak, 2903ft is about $1\frac{1}{4}$ miles north of the Glen Tarbert Road, and its main feature is the great east buttress which rises out of Garbh Coire Mor almost 1200ft to the summit. The Great Ridge and the Great Gully are obvious features with the two tiers of the south wall on the left which have some of the best routes on the mountain.

The North East Buttress is to the right of Pinnacle Ridge (see illustration) and this too is in the region of 1200ft. The buttress is divided into four tiers by three ledges or terraces. The third section is the famous Leac Mhor (Great Slab). This is some 500ft in height and up to 300ft wide. The best climbing is on the second and third tier.

Access

There are three ways to approach Garbh Bheinn. The easiest route from the south is via Corran Ferry (bus service from Glasgow and Fort William), or by road round Loch Eil from the Fort William Mallaig Road or by the road from Glenfinnan and Salen. The most popular way to reach the mountain from the road is by walking up Coir' an Iubhair, which has many good camp sites and which also affords the best views of the peak. One can also take the ridge on the left, up the slabs of Stron a'Garbh and follow the ridge along to the south side of Garbh Bheinn above Garbh Coire Mor. Though you miss the spectacular view of Garbh Bheinn this way, it is drier and is certainly a good route to return by. You can also motor further up Glen Tarbert to opposite Lochan a'Chothruim and ascend steeply to the southern slopes of Garbh Bheinn by way of Coire a'Chothruim. This Coire is not named on the 1 inch Tourist Map.

Camping/Accommodation

There are two hotels at Corran Ferry and camping is permissible in Coir' an Iubhair – a charge is made for this and permission should be obtained at Inversanda House. It is mainly hind

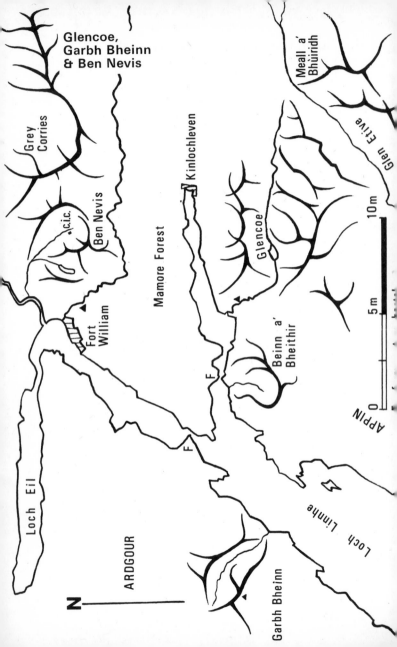

Glencoe,
Garbh Bheinn
& Ben Nevis

Grey
Corries

C.I.C.

Ben Nevis

Fort
William

Mamore Forest

Kinlochleven

Meall a'
Bhùiridh

Glen Etive

Glencoe

10 m

5 m

Beinn a'
Bheithir

APPIN

F

F

Loch Eil

ARDGOUR

N

Loch Linnhe

Garbh Bheinn

shooting in the Garbh Bheinn area and this extends from
1 September until approx. 15 February.

Map: Ben Nevis and Glencoe os 1 inch Tourist Map.

Guide Book: Glencoe and Ardgour. Volume II. *Glencoe, Beinn
Trilleachan, Garbh Bheinn inc. Bidean nam Bian and Aonach Eagach.*
L S Lovat scottish mountaineering trust

Mountain Rescue
Glencoe and Fort William Rescue Teams. Telephone Police
222 or 999.

Provisions
There is a shop on the Garbh Bheinn side of the ferry, open
most days.

86.1 Sgian Dubh
140ft grade iv** : fa *J R Marshall, L S Lovat 1956*
Towards l end of upper tier is a very obvious chimney with
crack at rear. Ascend to platform, 35ft, tr l and up ledges to
b st 40ft past platform. Go l and over overhang and take
groove to r and up nose then steep rock to exit near summit
cairn.

86.2 The Peeler
165ft grade −vi* : fa *J Moriarty, R Smith 1961*
Ascend edge of flake which borders first chimney of Sgian
Dubh. From platform (35ft) tr r to groove. (Pitch above
130ft.) Up groove and up l over small roof. Climb short, steep
crack (this falls back into a groove). Ascend further 60ft to top.

86.3 The Clasp
200ft grade −vi : fa *J R Marshall 1960*
On face of upper tier are some large overhangs. Under them
is a steep wall, which extends l below overhangs. Get onto
wall below r end of lowest overhang, slant up l to b; 40ft.
Continue up under roof, 20ft, then tr l 30ft to shallow groove.
Ascend chimney above, trend l to top.

86.4 **Brogue**

170ft grade v+**: FA *H MacInnes, M C MacInnes 1968*
Start at vertical crack/corner between Clasp and Scimitar.
Directly up on good holds to slabby section. Ascend to block
up R. Move L and gain ledge system and B on R. Climb wall
above slightly to L to top.

86.5 **Scimitar**

350ft grade v+***: FA *D D Stewart, D N Mill 1952*
Begin 100ft L of large boulder (see Butterknife) at a point (cairn)
where broken rocks run up R to long level shattered ledge
joining with Razor Slash and Butterknife. Ascend to shattered
ledge and from L edge direct up steep crack (spikes at vertical
section are good). An awkward R move is made on to smooth
slabs that lead to a B; 70ft. Easier climbing and a prominent
open chimney (crossed by slanting fracture of Razor Slash)
lead to Terrace. Follow directly above on upper tier by smooth
vertical groove to gain flake B on R. Go L by steep slabs (easier
above), to crest of Great Ridge.

86.6 **Razor Slash**

250ft grade −v**: FA *J R Marshall, L Lovat, A Hendry 1956*
Ascend large boulder mentioned in Butterknife. Go into Butterknife corner and up to ledge and B; 80ft. (This is past R edge
of shattered ledge going horizontally for some way.) TR L
horizontally, 25ft, along ledge to base of tapering gangway.
Ascend this and at top (crux) move out over nose, then R up
gradually L to B (loose spikes); 70ft. Then up by L slanting
fracture; this goes across obvious chimney of Scimitar to finish
on Terrace below upper tier.

86.7 **Butterknife**

350ft grade −v***: FA *J R Marshall, A Hendry, G Ritchie, I Haig
1956*
A large boulder is against the wall and immediately to R of
boulder is the prominent and continuous fracture line of route.
Climb this initially in the form of a chimney. Then by a corner
section to platform and B; 80ft. Next is a long steep crack, B at
40ft. Straight up to terrace, to a point below overhang on upper

86 The South Wall of The Great Ridge, Garbh Bheinn, Ardgour.
T=Terrace

tier near R end. Up overhang and in 100ft, reach area of final rocks of Great Ridge.

86.8 **Bealach Buttress**
350ft grade IV** : FA *D D Stewart, D N Mill 1952*
From cairn at lowest rocks follow easiest line to sharp arete at top, or finish up corner as shown on photograph.

86.GR **The Great Ridge**
1000ft grade III*** : FA *J H Bell, W Brown 1897*
Approach is by Garbh Choire Mor. Directly under the Great Ridge a band of slabs is crossed by two grass rakes. Ascend lower rake by slabs and grass close to Great Gully, or (more easily) by following first gully of South East Chimney route and then TR R to lower rake. Along rake (downwards) to foot of Ridge. The first 200ft give the best climbing. The climb finishes just below the summit cairn.

Winter Severe ($1\frac{1}{2}$–3 hours)*** An excellent winter line.

87.1 **Route I**
110ft grade III* : FA *J K W Dunn, A M MacAlpine, W H Murray 1936*
Begin at bottom rocks at S end of buttress (same start as Route II). Climb is rather indefinite. Ascend 250ft by slabs and walls up initial section to first terrace. Walk up to main face near SE end of buttress. 40ft up slabs to L end of a ledge, this goes R across face. Follow ledge, bearing R by series of corners to second terrace; 270ft. 200ft of slab at R end of Leac Mhor leads to third terrace. Climb buttress by any line above.

87.2 **Route II**
110ft grade IV** : FA *B K Barber, J Lomas 1939*
Same start to first terrace. From cairn up 40ft to R-running ledge of Route I and follow straight up avoiding L trend. Turn overhang at top of tier by long R TR and reach second terrace. Second terrace dips from R to L below big slab of Leac Mhor. Top of slab has a bristling band of rock (Route I on this tier is far to R). Landmark for route is narrow chimney which cuts

87 North East Buttress, Garbh Bheinn, Ardgour. lm=Leac Mhor. The terraces on the routes are obvious on photograph

Leac Mhor, starting up not far L of arrival point on second terrace. Chimney goes directly up for 170ft to small recess. The original line is up the chimney to a shaky block; 150ft. Grooves go R across slab bending gradually up to ST and B under a short overhang – otherwise the run-out will be 150ft. Up overhang (good holds) and slant R up slabs, skirting round overhanging band. Take easiest line to third terrace.

Turret Variation:
Grade IV*: FA *D D Stewart, D N Mill 1952*
Up original line to top of short overhang; instead of going R to avoid overhanging belt, do easy L TR into grassy niche below Turret. Go L round nose (exposed) and directly up Turret on steep rock (good holds).

Variation:
Grade V+*: FA *G Shields, T Low, W Nelson 1954*
Take original line to top of short overhang and climb R round foot of overhanging belt for 20ft. Up overhang by long upward step on to a sloping hold utilising a tiny side hand-hold. Continue up to B at 60ft and end up fine airy arete.

Direct Finish:
Grade V*: FA *L S Lovat, D C Hutcheson; D Scott, Miss E Stark 1954*
Up original route all the way up chimney to the small recess at 170ft. (The figure 2 on illustration also marks the recess.) Ascend a grey slab on L of recess slanting L to its crest. Go L into a groove. Up groove 50ft to a narrow ledge (rock finger B). TR L a few ft and up steep L side of rock band base of obvious diedre. Up this followed by steep rock to third terrace.

88 On the excellent rock of the South Wall of Garbh Bheinn Great Ridge. Brogue (Upper Tier). Ballachulish narrows and the peaks of Glencoe behind

Ben Nevis, General

At 4406ft Ben Nevis is the highest peak in the British Isles and though it looks somewhat undignified as seen from Fort William, its northerly cliffs offer some of the best climbing in the country.

In winter the gullies are alpine in character and the more difficult climbs can be formidable undertakings especially early in the year with limited daylight.

The name Nevis is somewhat obscure but one theory is that it may mean 'venomous one', a name not unapplicable to those who have been caught in a winter storm on that peak. The northwest spur of Ben Nevis is Carn Dearg, 3961ft – this is the great mass of rock on your right as you ascend the Allt a'Mhuilinn, and on the Great Buttress of this peak are some of the finest rock climbs in Scotland.

The main features of the Ben Nevis cliffs are North East Buttress on the left and in the centre, Tower Ridge, and on the right, as mentioned, Carn Dearg Buttress. Between these ridges and many subsidiary buttresses are the gullies and these are numbered from left to right as you look onto the face.

Beyond the Charles Inglis Clark Hut (2200ft above sea level) the Allt a'Mhuilinn rises in Coire Leis, above which is the Carn Mor Dearg Arete which does not fall below 3475ft and connects Ben Nevis with Carn Mor Dearg. This affords a popular route back down to the CIC Hut from the summit – and also a dangerous one should there be much ice – and abseil posts (MR 171711) at 50ft intervals have been erected to expedite descent in bad conditions. Keep the route markers to your L going down to Arete from summit. Carn Mor Dearg offers the best vantage point to view the Ben Nevis cliffs. From the Arete a further route leads down to Glen Nevis, but care should be taken in bad conditions as there have been several serious accidents due to people going too far to the east here. The proper route is shown on the photograph of the southern aspect of Ben Nevis.

Getting off the summit in bad visibility in winter can be difficult. If one wishes to return to the CIC Hut the CARN MOR DEARG ARETE DESCENT IS NOT RECOM-MENDED. Gullies 3 and 4 afford the best means of descent provided they can be correctly located (marker at top of Gully 4). Gully 3 has a small pinnacle at top. If in doubt return by the tourist path. Don't go without a map and compass and study the topography of the mountain during clear weather. Ben Nevis can be extremely treacherous in winter and climbing on it, especially in winter, should be treated seriously.

Access

There is a good BR sleeper service to Fort William from King's Cross and bus services from Inverness, Glasgow (via Glencoe). Ben Nevis is bounded on the south and west by Glen Nevis. The Glen Nevis road winds its way up the Glen to a large car park below the long waterslabs of the southern slopes of the Ben. A path continues from here up the true right of the Water of Nevis to Steall Hut which is the property of the Junior Mountaineering Club of Scotland (Lochaber Section), see photograph.

The car park at the head of the Glen Nevis road is also a starting point for ascending to the Carn Mor Dearg Arete. This provides an attractive and easy route to the summit and also enables one to climb on the East Face of North East Buttress in winter by descending into Coire Leis.

Just east of where the road crosses the Water of Nevis at the Polldubh Bridge are the Polldubh Crags, which afford pleasant short climbs on an off day.

The Youth Hostel is situated some three miles up Glen Nevis from Fort William and opposite this is a footbridge which gives access to the main tourist path some 500ft directly up the hillside. This path is rather boggy except during frosty weather or droughts and the better route is from Achintee Farm on the Ben Nevis side of the river. Going out of Fort William on the Inverness Road the Glen Nevis Road is on the right just short of the main road bridge over the Nevis and the Achintee road is first right on the Inverness side of the bridge and one bears right again at the shop a few hundred yards up this road.

The tourist track goes all the way to the summit of Ben Nevis from Achintee Farm, skirting the face of Meall an Suidhe. This route, as far as the halfway point up Ben Nevis, is also used to reach the CIC Hut, owned by the S.M.C. Instead of continuing up the path beyond Lochan Meall an t-Suidhe by the Red Burn the route strikes off to the North across the fairly flat section of moor from a small cairn on the main tourist track, above the Lochan on the eastern side. Beyond the deer fence the path veers right and descends slightly to the Allt a'Mhuilinn. The hut is situated close to this stream just above the junction of the stream from Lochan na Ciste. From Achintee to the hut with a rucksack takes a little over two hours.

A further route is from the Ben Nevis Distillery, opposite the Mallaig/Inverness road junction, approx. $2\frac{1}{2}$ miles from Fort William. A path leads from behind the Distillery, across the main railway line, following the small stream to join up with a narrow gauge railway line above. Follow this to the left for a few hundred yards and cross a small bridge. Climb up the slope diagonally to the right to reach the Allt a'Mhuilinn near the small dam of the British Aluminium Company. Follow the stream on the NE Bank to the hut (reasonable path). Time approx. 2–4 hours depending on conditions.

A Forestry Commission road now goes up to the small dam on the Allt a'Mhuilinn from Torlundy and the Forestry Commission should be asked for permission to use it.
The other route from Glen Nevis over the Carn Mor Dearg Arete is short and dry, but is only suitable for doing climbs on the eastern flanks of the mountain.

Camping/Accommodation
There are plenty of hotels in Fort William and guest houses and there is a Youth Hostel in Glen Nevis. The Steall Hut and the CIC Hut are open to members of affiliated clubs, though there can be difficulty at weekends especially in winter at the CIC due to popular demand. There is good camping in Glen Nevis (various points) and there are a number of camp sites above the small dam on the Allt a'Mhuilinn – right up to the CIC Hut. Above the hut there are also some good sites, especially in one of the hollows some 200yds south west of the hut by a spring.

Map: OS 1 inch Ben Nevis and Glencoe Tourist Map.

Guide Books: Ben Nevis J R Marshall SCOTTISH MOUNTAINEERING TRUST. *Guide to Winter Climbs, Ben Nevis and Glencoe* Ian Clough.

Mountain Rescue
A stretcher is kept at the CIC Hut with First Aid equipment (official MR post). Ask locally regarding communication from the CIC Hut, e.g. radio/telephone etc. Help can also be obtained by telephoning from either the Distillery or from Glen Nevis Youth Hostel or Glen Nevis Farm. Rescue Team/s Lochaber Mountaineering Club, Police Fort William 2361

or 999. Steall Hut is also a MR Post, but this will only be available if someone is in residence. There are two Shelters, one is on Carn Dearg MR 158719 and the other in Coire Leis MR 173714, these are for emergency use only.

Provisions
There are many shops in Fort William; maps, guide books, etc., can be purchased, as well as climbing equipment. Early closing day Wednesday.

90.a Italian Climb
600ft Winter, Severe (4–7 hours)** : FA *J Marshall, A Mac-Corquodale, G Ritchie February 1958*
There is a deep gully with an obvious two-tier rib on L, on W side of Tower Ridge. This climb follows the gully with two main ice pitches followed by a slanting TR R across face to reach crest of Tower Ridge under Little Tower.

90.a Garadh Gully
400ft Winter, Very Difficult (3½ hours) : FA *unrecorded*
This gully gives (usually) two steep ice pitches, 50ft and 40ft. Start just above and R of Italian Climb.

90 b–b Gully 3 Buttress
500ft Winter, Hard–Very Difficult (2–4 hours)*** : FA *L S Lovat, D J Bennet February 1957*
An obvious buttress projects into coire on L and under narrow part of Gully 3. Two thirds way up buttress is an obvious platform. From big snow bay under prow of buttress climb to platform. Grooves lead up L, and a steep corner gives a good finish.

89 Opposite: The South side of Ben Nevis from Steall Hut, Glen Nevis. The route line marks route to Carn Mor Dearg Arete (a), keeping to the true L of the stream at start. SG = Steall Gully, a 700ft winter climb of very difficult standard, straightforward. A = Abseil Posts

90 Overleaf left: A view of the Ben Nevis cliffs from the CIC Hut. Top left is NE Buttress. z = Zero Gully. O = Observatory Ridge. ·5 = Point Five Gully. Ob = Observatory Buttress. DB = Douglas Boulder. GT = Great Tower. 2 = Gully 2. c = Comb Gully. Cb = The Comb

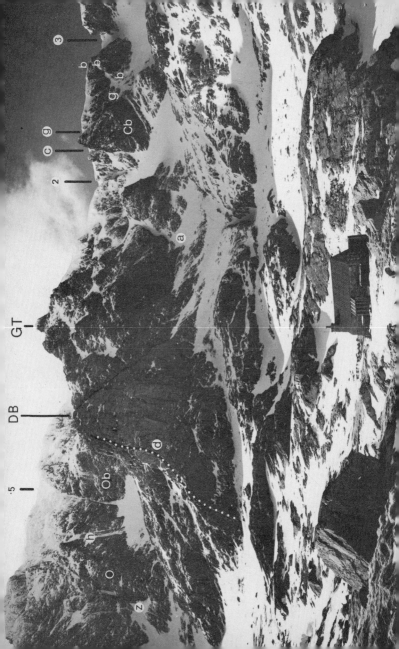

90.d **Direct Route**

800ft grade III: FA *W Brown, L Hinxman, H Raeburn, W Douglas 1896*

As seen from bottom of Route 1, the route follows skyline directly upwards from lowest rocks. It forms the longest direct line up ridge; much variation possible.

90.g **Green Gully**

400ft Winter, Hard Severe (3–5 hours): FA *J H Bell, J Henson, R Morsley, P Small 4 April 1937*

This gully flanks the Comb on the Carn Dearg side. Near the start there is an ice chimney, on the L are the steep cliffs of the Comb. Shortly after this gully steepens (steep walls either side) and some easier pitches lead to 60ft ice pitch, followed by another steep ice wall. Next section fairly easy to bottom of final difficulties, a pitch usually climbed up R corner of wall. Finish up snow scoop.

90.h **West Face, Lower Route**

800ft Winter, Very Severe (5–7 hours): FA *J R Marshall, T W Patey, W D Brooker (through leads) February 1959*

Up long point of ice L of tongue of snow below Point Five Gully. TR L on face and up 3 pitches on ice-covered rock of 60–80ft. Reach steep snow niches 200ft below ridge crest. Return R along face (ascending line with continuous vertical wall above). This involves 3 more pitches 80–100ft, the second has a tension-TR and third a fine ice chimney. From this point (about 500ft up) route is easier and broad snow gully to immediate R of Observatory Ridge is climbed, finishing by ridge near top.

90.3 **Gully 3**

300ft Winter, Moderate (2 hours from hut to top)

This is an easy gully rising from Coire na Ciste. No pitches, but quite steep. Top section is divided by pinnacle (visible from hut). L side is easier. This gully together with Gully 4 provide good descent routes, but if in doubt, in bad visibility, descend by tourist path.

---

91 Previous page right: Looking along Carn Mor Dearg Arete, showing A=Abseil posts. This photograph was taken in mid-May.

92.1 **Route Major**

1000ft Winter, Mild Severe (3–5 hours)*** : FA *I Clough,
H MacInnes (through leads) February 1969*
This very long route involves considerable route finding. Start
at lowest point of rocks and follow route line on illustration.
Frostbite is crossed at the broad snow ledge and the upper
section of the route, though looking formidable, is straightforward with a number of exposed TR.

92.2 **Frostbite**

900ft Winter, Severe (5–7 hours) : FA *I Clough, D Pipes,
J Alexander, P Hannon, M Buck February 1958*
Start from same snow bay as Slalom and take ice groove to R to
reach 400ft snowfield. Up this R and cross rock ridge below nose
of Central Spur proper to reach further snow slopes trending R
under Spur. Go out R onto NE on these and finish by Man Trap.
(See North East Buttress.)

92.3 **Slalom**

900ft Winter, Very Difficult (4 hours)*** : FA *D Pipes, I Clough
(alt. leads), R. Shaw, J M Alexander, A Flegg January 1959*
Route rises towards Central Spur, zig-zags to avoid rock walls.
It is separated from Frostbite by rock ridge and runs parallel.
Below spur TR 100ft L, easy snow slope leads to final rocks overlooking Cresta Gully and just L of Central Spur (rocks crux),
easy climbing from top.

92.4 **Cresta Climb**

900ft Winter, Very Difficult (3–5 hours)** : FA *T W Patey,
L S Lovat, A G Nicol February 1957*
Start to L of rocky spur, and 100ft R of Bob-run. Iced rocks (or
ice) are climbed to reach broad snowshelf. A small gully leads
up R side of shelf to couloir. Follow couloir to top in ice basin.
TR up R to easy snow slope to finish.

92 *Overleaf left:* Carn Mor Dearg Arete and East Face, North East
Buttress. A=Abseil posts (descent to Coire Leis). FP=First
Platform, the easy snow ramp from Coire Leis is obvious. NEB=
North East Buttress. OR=Observatory Ridge. GT=Great Tower,
Tower Ridge

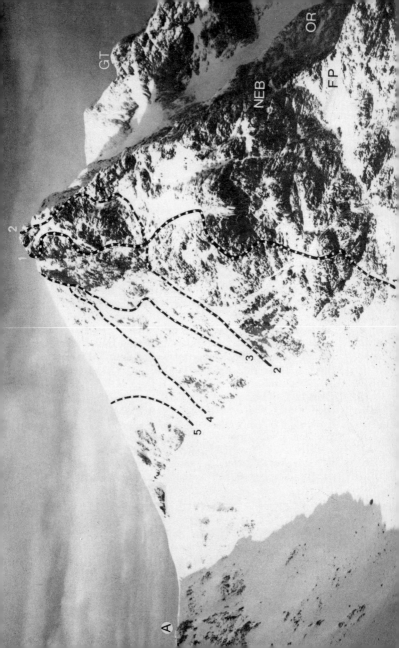

92.5 **Bob-run**

400ft Winter, Difficult (1½–3 hours) : FA *I Clough, D Pipes and party February 1959*
Start almost level with Carn Mor Dearg Arete Col. Route takes a couloir at L side of face. Start to R of buttress and climb 100ft of ice or iced rocks to gain couloir. In a further 100ft the route trends L. Two variations above, with usually one ice pitch in each.

94SC **Slingsby's Chimney**

400ft grade II* : FA *G Hastings, H Priestman, W C Slingsby 1895*
An easy access route to start North East Buttress exiting just above First Platform.

Winter Very Difficult (1–2 hours)* : FA *Unknown*
When this is done in conjunction with North East Buttress it makes a very long climb. The route can be done to First Platform with descent down sloping shelf to Coire Leis as a short day climb.

94 **Raeburn's 18-Minute Route**

450ft grade II : FA *H Raeburn, Dr and Mrs Inglis Clark 1901*
Start 20ft L of Slingsby's Chimney and up L wall of gully.

94 **Platform Rib**

700ft grade IV* (4–6 hours) : FA *J H B Bell, C M Allan, M Stewart 1934;*
FA (Winter) *H MacInnes, I Clough, T Sullivan (through leads), M White March 1959*
50ft R of Slingsby's Chimney is a deep black chimney. The rock rib forming L wall is climbed after ascending a few feet in chimney. Go up rib mostly on rib (short sections in chimney). An easy chimney at top leads to North East Buttress, 100ft above First Platform.

Winter Very Severe (3–6 hours)
An overhang may require direct aid in winter. Keep mainly to summer line.

93 *Previous page right:* On the Upper Section, Route Major, Ben Nevis. Carn Mor Dearg Arete below

94 *Opposite:* North East Buttress, Ben Nevis, with the Orion Face and the Minus gullies. Z=Zero Gully. G=Gardyloo Gully

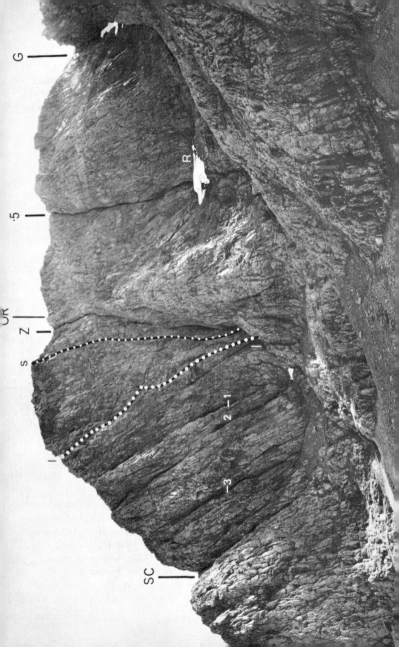

94.2 Minus Two Gully

900ft grade v+ : FA *W Peascod, B L Dodson 1950*

This is the second gully to L of Zero Gully. Easy for 100ft. A further 80ft to cave. Climb out and over chockstone to ST and B; 35ft. A harder chimney to ST poor B under a long chimney and groove with big black overhang above; 30ft. Up overhang and move round edge on L to ST and B (hard); 80ft. Up chimneys for 200ft to base of series of steep greasy chimneys. Climb these as direct as possible; the second, by a vertical L wall until step enables a move back into true bed, above overhang. The chimneys finish against wall, B on L; 100ft. Up crack on L to where gully opens out. Two lines from here: either a chimney (easy angle) on L, or a continuation to R by number of bulging chimneys; 70ft. Awkward overhanging chimneys lead to easier ground and main ridge (North East Buttress).

Winter Very Severe, SERIOUS (8 hours) : FA *J R Marshall, J Stenhouse, D Haston*

This takes approx. the summer line, a very serious climb.

94 Minus One Buttress, North Eastern Grooves

970ft grade v+* : FA *R Downs, M O'Hara, E Langmuir*

This climb generally follows obvious crack line bottom R to top L of Minus One Buttress. Over halfway up are a series of overhangs turned by moving onto Minus Two Buttress and regain crack line above. Start near centre of buttress, below R-angled corner at 50ft. Up into R-angled corner, to platform on R; 70ft. Above L is triangular flake. Climb this by crack on R using sling. Go diagonally L then direct to big plinth; 225ft. Move L into damp groove, up for 75ft. Turn overhang by TR L (above ST) below steep nose until possible to ascend. Reach large ledges, level with overhangs on R. Down into Minus Two Gully and up easy rocks opposite. Reach glacis where gully eases. Cairn (575ft). TR obvious line R, back onto Minus One Buttress (hard start). Up to perched blocks; pass and up chimney groove on R (continuation of lower line); 30ft. Move R along ledge to open buttress crest above overhangs, runner, bridge (strenuous) up groove to big terrace. Up 40ft pinnacle. Easily for 100ft to leaning pedestal. Sharp arete makes finish, joining North East Buttress above Second Platform.

94 **Astronomy**

955ft grade v* : FA *I Clough, G Grandison 1962*
Follow line of cracks and grooves parallel to and R of Minus
One Gully. Starts from grassy ledge about 50ft R of foot of
Minus One Gully. Move diagonally R to slabby crest and
follow grassy grooves to flake belays; 120ft. Up, then R, to
large spike B below twin grooves; 65ft. Climb R hand groove,
then trend R to corner bounding the Great Slab Rib on its L;
up corner to spike B; 120ft. Continue up corner, TR L to
chockstone B smooth groove (junction with Minus One Gully's
'avoiding' pitches); 80ft. Up cracks to B at foot of big slab
corner. Up crack in slab to ST and chockstone B; 60ft & 50ft.
Up flake chimney and corner above to B; 70ft. Minus One
Gully now trends back to gully proper. Up for 15ft, TR R climb
groove to ST below overhang; P B; 70ft. Turn overhang on R and
follow crack to overhung corner; 35ft. The overhanging crack
on L was climbed by second man but leader traversed round
corner R 20ft until possible to trend L again to rejoin crack
line; P B 85ft. Break out L and continue more easily to grass
ledges and chockstone B; 130ft. TR L up to grassy corner and
continue L to crest of North East Buttress; 70ft.

Winter Very Severe, SERIOUS (5–9 hours) : FA *K Spence,
A Fyffe, H MacInnes (alt. leads).*
The winter line took almost the same one as summer.

94.1 **Long Climb**

1150ft grade —v** : FA *J H Bell, J Wilson 1940*
Up easy ochre coloured rib on L of Zero Gully to gain a small
ledge, 200ft. From L of ledge a rib leads steeply up to base of
'great slab rib', (a prominent feature). Go round rib on L and
up to gain base of 'great slab rib'; 150ft. (Or, climb rib direct,
or climb by groove on R side of rib – harder than original route,
with difficulties in lower rocks.) TR R onto crest of 'great slab
rib' and up by parallel cracks to gain a recess, B, 100ft. Go out
and up to R and climb more easily to 'the basin'; 150ft. Cross
'basin' and climb to base of 'second slab rib'; 120ft.
Up rib by slab edge, high up a steep section is turned by L wall
(climbed direct v+) to regain crest, 100ft B. The wall above
is turned on L or R and is awkward ST B 30ft. The route is now
easier with variations. Original route slants up L for base of a
further great slab approx. 200ft. high. The rocks to R of this

are taken to a niche near the top, and a short difficult pitch leads to top of slab. Easier then to top of North East Buttress.

94.s Slav Route

1000ft grade −v*: FA *E Derzag, M Debelak, E Wedderburn 1934*
Start from rock rib next to Zero Gully. Up to ST and B; 50ft. Up R then L in easy chimney; 65ft. Move R to edge of steep slab above gully, then up and back to L to ledge; 45ft. Up shallow scoop on L, with small cave and small waterfall at top. B on ledge; 50ft. Direct up from R of ledge to P; 45ft. Keep to edge of Zero for several hundred feet; above route goes closer to gully. Near top, route slants L, up chimneys and corners. Top is reached round corner of North East Buttress.

94.OR Observatory Ridge, Ordinary Route

900ft grade II*: FA *H Raeburn 1901*
Route starts at base of rocks and follows the crest (more or less). It is possible to go from Observatory Gully in a TR to L to gain Ridge above lowest rocks. Steep parts can be turned on R. Finish in steep buttress with big square-cut rocks.

Winter Severe (4–6 hours)***: FA *H Raeburn, F Goggs, W Mounsey April 1920*
Possibly the hardest of the classic ridges of Ben Nevis. The lowest buttress usually gives the hardest problems. Gain a shelf on L side one third way up this buttress then slant R to crest. Difficulties can be turned above this, and Zero Gully can be climbed for the last 500ft if time is short.

94.·5 Point Five Gully

1000ft grade v+*: FA *M Noon, G MacIntosh 1955*
(1) Climb gully to ledge B on L; 110ft. (2) Continue up gully until awkward move must be made to R on to overhanging groove. Climb this and TR L. Several mantelshelves lead to good ledge (P B); 120ft. (3) Climb direct to overhang. Move R on small holds to rib. Up this and L into gully. Climb steep wall on R to another rib, followed to small spike B. Crux; 120ft. (4) Up rib to block B on R; 20ft. (5) Go L and climb chimney; 120ft. (6) To B on R; 20ft. (7) Short overhanging walls above are climbed; 120ft. (8) Climb gully to large ledge, B on L; 120ft. (9) Continue up to small scoop, no B; 120ft. (10) Climb scoop to ledge; 50ft. (11) The steep chimney above climbed to

chockstone, then up outer edge; 6oft. Easy climbing leads to top; 4ooft.

Winter route see 95.·5.

94. R Rubicon Wall

4ooft grade —v** : FA *A T Hargreaves, F Heap, R Heap 1933*
Start from L edge of ledge, above yellow slabs on L of buttress. Up groove in rib then L then up to B; 6oft. Go R of ledge, up small gully to ledge and B; 40ft. TR horizontally R, 50ft to gully, up this and cross to step over R wall to B; 9oft. A horizontal TR across face and small buttress leads to v corner. From its R go onto face and up to ledges, then up shallow corner to ridge on L, B; 6oft. Take groove or ridge to B; 2oft. From R end of B ledge gain higher ledge up and L up crack to wall then L and up small groove to B at top of rib; 6oft. Up L corner to ledges and B; 40ft. Up grooves and reach rib on R and ledge. Up blocks to recess. Move to R to ledge, B; 8oft. Go up and into corner on R with big block and easy slab. Up corner to L to easier ground. Easier to top.

95. NEB North East Buttress

1oooft grade III*** : FA *J E Hopkinson, B Hopkinson 1892*
This can be ascended from the broad, easy ledge which runs up to the First Platform from the E. Or, take one of the routes described in text to First Platform (in summer). Follow up narrow ridge above First Platform to steeper section, climb direct (IV), or take ledge R to shallow gully trending back L to Second Platform (small), or go L of steeper section to slanting stony gully and trend back R above. Continue several hundred ft above Second Platform to smooth overhanging wall. Up corner steps on R (or take direct). Short way above is the Man Trap, a 1oft rock nose. Follow nail marks. Easy above to top.

Winter Very Difficult–Severe (4–6 hours)*** : FA *unrecorded*
Gain First Platform (usually by rising TR from E). On the steeper rocks of the crest above TR ledge on R to gully, leading back L to gain Second Platform. Take more or less the summer route to Man Trap. This can be turned on R by short descent and TR to scoop. This leads to base of steep corner, which can also be hard (it may be better to move down and L to near top of Man Trap; a shallow chimney goes up L of ridge crest on easier terrain). It is also possible to turn the Man Trap by descending and moving E then up.

95 **The Orion Face** (direct line)

1400ft Winter, Very Severe, SERIOUS (6–10 hours) : FA
R Smith, J Marshall (through leads) February 1960

Take the direct line which starts from the broad ledge of Slav
Route. This is reached after 100ft of ice climbing. Follow an ice
groove beside Beta Route to P B below a roof. Make a L TR to
the Basin. Snow and ice climbing leads to base of second slab
rib. This is turned by ice wall on R. L slanting ice and snow
grooves lead to snow slopes below last tower of North East
Buttress. Ice grooves lead to summit slopes.

95.Z **Zero Gully**

1000ft Winter, Very Severe, SERIOUS (3–6 hours) : FA
H MacInnes, T W Patey (alt. leads), G Nicol February 1957

First 400ft very steep, few belays (dead man B may be useful)
which makes this a potentially dangerous climb. Upper section
of climb is easy.

95.·5 **Point Five Gully**

1000ft Winter, Very Severe, SERIOUS (5–8 hours) : FA
*J Alexander, I Clough, D Pipes, R Shaw (alt. leads). This ascent was
done over period of five days. Completed 16 January 1959*

(1) Up steep ice-covered slab to bolt B (in place) on L wall;
40–100ft. (2) Up to groove on L of ice bulge (some P in place).
Surmount bulge on R; 6oft for ST and P B 25ft higher. (3)
Difficult ice bulge followed by vertical pitch in narrowing
chimney to ST and P B (in place) at foot of tight chimney; 60ft.
(4) Up chimney, then easier climbing (apart from 10 ft bulge)
to ST and P B; 60ft. (5) Up to foot of cave pitch. Bolt B (in place)
on L wall; 35ft. (6) Climb a steepening ice pitch; vertical at top.
Difficult exit to snow slope, P B on R; 45ft. Easily up snow 100ft.
20ft awkward ice-covered rocks climbed L to R. 500ft of
climbing involving one small steep pitch and a strenuous ice
chimney leads to top.

Summer route see 94.·5.

95 North East Buttress, Ben Nevis. a=slope from summit to Carn
Mor Dearg Arete. m=Man Trap (crux of North East Buttress).
1=First Platform, showing the easy traverse line from Coire Leis
on left. −3=Minus Three Gully. 2=Slav Route. OR=
Observatory Ridge

95.F Good Friday Climb

500ft Winter, Very Difficult (2–4 hours)***: FA *G G Macphee, R W Lovel, H Shepherd, D Edwards April 1939*

Start of climb is at head of Observatory Gully and below Gardyloo Gully (see Gardyloo Gully for start). To L a snow shelf runs out to top of Observatory Buttress and a gully is taken for 240ft until blocked by wall. Go R then back L up further gully system to top. Upper section, which is steep, can be hard when icy.

97.OB Observatory Buttress, Ordinary Route

650ft grade −IV*: FA *H Raeburn 1902*

This Buttress is to R of Point Five Gully. Starts up easiest section of face, near centre, just round to R of bulge and up steep rocks towards an apparent hollow in protruding section of rock above. 30ft up first pitch to small ledge, B. TR up to R, then back L to big ledge, B; 70ft. Up to big B in large square corner; 60ft. Go to R for a few ft then slant up L to corner (B high on wall); 60ft. Up to R close to gully, then direct to B behind block (thread); 50ft. Direct up groove for a few ft, then TR R. Move (crux), from smooth slab across chimney to big ledge. A further 300ft of easy climbing to top.

97.G Gardyloo Gully

400ft Winter, Severe (2–4 hours): FA *G Hastings, W Haskett-Smith April 1897*

Conditions and difficulty depend on build up of snow; most pitches are usually covered and it is easy as far as the through route – there is sometimes a tunnel under the chockstone – but usually the R of this has to be climbed. Continue up on steep snow or ice to cornice (often double) which can be awkward.

96 Opposite: Looking up Point Five Gully, Ben Nevis. Pitches 3 and 4 above

97 Overleaf: Tower Ridge, Ben Nevis. OR=Observatory Ridge. OB= Observatory Buttress. F=start of Good Friday Climb. ET=Eastern Traverse. E=Echo Wall. DB=Douglas Boulder. g=Garadh Gully. 2=Gully 2. c=Comb Gully.

97.1 **Tower Gully**

350ft Winter, Easy–Difficult: FA *G Hastings, E Haskett-Smith, W Haskett-Smith April 1897*

An easy walk in summer, and usually an even snow slope in winter, though there can be ice in severe conditions. Cornice sometimes has to be tunnelled.

97.a **Tower Ridge**

1900ft grade II***: FA (Winter) *N Collie, G Solly, J Collier March 1894*

Though a route up the face of the Douglas Boulder (700ft) should be included in an ascent of the ridge, many people now by-pass the Boulder by the eastern gully leading to Douglas Gap. This is marked on photograph. It is not always easy to locate gully in misty weather as its base merges with the broad rocky slope, but the bay should be found. From gap an easy chimney slants L to give access to ridge crest. Ridge is fairly level and narrow and steepens to small pitch with overhanging wall. Climb up to and along ledge running R. Easy scrambling above. Two small gaps are crossed. 160ft beyond second gap, base of Little Tower is reached. Normal route is up rocks on L. Also a route direct to top. Easy to Great Tower base. The ridge crest goes to its NE corner. Keep to E, on grassy ledge (Eastern TR), to foot of through route formed by big block, up to steep easy rocks on R to summit of Tower. Descend to Tower Gap, cross, and follow to steep small buttress, turned on R by a chimney, or easier rock W.

Winter Very Difficult (3–10 hours)
The summer route is followed approx. Care should be taken at the exposed section above Echo Wall at the Little Tower. The Eastern Traverse is the obvious ledge running L of onset of Great Tower (see illustration).

98.PB **Pinnacle Buttress of the Tower**

500ft Winter, Very Difficult (1½–3 hours): FA *D J Bennet, A Tait 1957*

From the Garadh ascend by L up shallow snow gully about 150ft, then R along easy ledge. Above, crest of buttress rises in steep ridge with easier rocks either side. Route goes R of crest over snow and ice-covered rock. A snow-filled groove is climbed; 60ft approx. Then R TR of 40ft to another groove followed straight up until easy rocks lead L to top of buttress, below Great Tower. This part goes up midway between crest of Buttress and Glover's Chimney.

98. GC **Glover's Chimney** (Tower Gap W. Chimney)

Winter, Hard Severe (2–6 hours) : FA *G Graham Macphee, G Williams, D Henderson March 1935*

This is Tower Gap W. Chimney and starts from Garadh na Ciste to R of Pinnacle Buttress route and goes directly to Tower Gap via the narrow gully. Choose the line of least resistance. Crux is usually final chimney and can be climbed on L or R walls. 150ft of rope recommended due to lack of suitable ST. Climb finishes at Tower Gap.

99. sg **South Gully**

400ft Difficult (1–2 hours to top from hut)* : FA (Winter) *G Graham Macphee April 1936*

Climb from foot of narrow section of Gully 3, level with lowest part of Gully 3 Buttress. Go to the R up prominent steep angled ledge to foot of gully. Gully goes back up L. Finish near highest part of Creag Coire na Ciste. Cornice can be difficult.

99. ng **North Gully** (Creag Coire na Ciste)

350ft Very Difficult (1½–2 hours to top from hut) : FA (Winter) *J Y MacDonald, H W Turnbull March 1934*

To the L of Gully 4 and just below a thin steep black buttress is a couloir. Crux is where couloir narrows and steepens, and vertical ice pitch 12–14ft is climbed (this pitch can be 100ft sometimes). Moderate snow leads to foot of black buttress. Keep to R past this and snow slope leads to summit.

98 *Opposite:* Tower Ridge, West Face, looking over Garadh na Ciste. A=Carn Mor Dearg Arete. PB=Pinnacle Buttress. GT=Great Tower. Circles denote climbers, one of whom is crossing Tower Gap.

99 *Overleaf:* Looking across to Carn Dearg and the cliffs of Ben Nevis. NEB=North East Buttress. z=Zero Gully. o=Observatory Ridge. ·5=Point Five Gully. g=Gardyloo Gully. l=Tower Gully. GT= Great Tower. DB=Douglas Boulder. a=approach to Douglas Boulder. 2=Gully 2. c=Comb Gully. 3=Gully 3. ct=Start of Curtain climb. b=Carn Dearg Buttress. s=South Castle Gully. n=North Castle Gully. CR=Castle Ridge

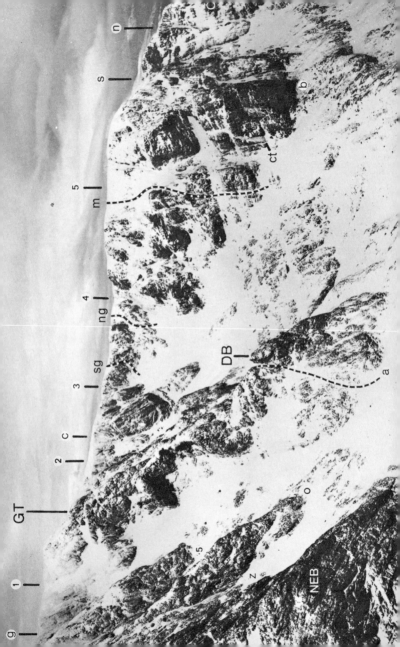

99.4 **Gully 4**

400ft Winter, Easy (2 hours from hut to top)* :
See location from photograph : One of the easiest of the gullies,
though sometimes there is a cornice. An easy descent route (at
present, marker at top of gully).

99 **Gully 4 Buttress**

Very Difficult (2 hours from hut to top) : FA (Winter) *J H B
Bell, R Elton 1929*
The buttress on the N between Gully 4 and Trident gives
moderate climbing to summit of Carn Dearg.

99.m **Moonlight Gully**

500ft Winter, Difficult (2 hours from hut)* : FA *W Inglis Clark,
T Gibson January 1898*
L of Gully 5, Moonlight Gully Buttress separates Gully 5 from
Moonlight Gully. The gully is direct and narrow.

99.5 **Gully 5**

1500ft Winter, Easy–Difficult (2 hours from hut to top)*
A straightforward snow climb, see photograph.

99.ct **The Curtain**

300ft Winter, Very Severe (4–6 hours) : FA *J Knight, D Bathgate
February 1965*
This is the big slab-corner in upper L side of Great Buttress.
In winter it forms a great curtain of ice.

100.1 **Gully 2 Buttress**

400ft Severe (2–3 hours)** : FA *J Marshall, L Lovat, A Hendry
March 1958*
Up steep snow and occasionally iced rocks to shelf below steep
upper wall. A short hard ice pitch leads to easier snow above.

100.2 **Gully 2**

400ft Winter, Mild Severe (1½–2 hours)* : FA *J Collier,
G Hastings, W Slingsby 1896 (Easter)*
This gully is situated between the cliffs which merge with
Tower Ridge and the Comb. It cuts deeply into the cliffs. The
climb is easier when banked-up with snow; if not, the Great
Pitch can present difficulties. There is often a large cornice.

100 Overleaf: Looking into Gully 2. The two climbers at cornice
indicate scale

100.3 Comb Gully

450ft Winter, Hard Severe (2–5 hours)*** : FA *F Stangle, R Morsley, P A Small April 1938*

Early in winter this gully may be hard with steep ice in upper section.

103,1,2,3 These three gullies were climbed by *I Clough, P Nicholson, D Pipes April 1958*

Colando Gully

600ft Winter, Difficult ($\frac{1}{2}$–1 hour)

The L Gully, no difficulties.

Arch Gully

600ft Winter, Difficult ($\frac{1}{2}$–1 hour)

This gully has big arch block half way up, steep.

Surprise Gully

550ft Winter, Very Difficult (1–1$\frac{1}{2}$ hours)

This leads by broken rocks to a shoulder and by ice groove on L.

103.4 Cousin's Buttress: Ordinary Route

Winter, Severe (4–6 hours) : FA *C H C Brunton, J Clarkson February 1957*

Ascend the approach gully (one short ice pitch) to a point level with top of Cousin's Buttress then TR on steep snow to large ice fall. Climb R edge of this – steep for 100ft. to easier angled snow to upper basin. Choice of routes to summit.

103.6 Waterfall Gully

700ft Winter, Very Severe (4–6 hours)* : FA *D Pipes, I Clough, J Alexander, R Shaw, A Fleg (shared leads) January 1959*

This gully is just R of Great Buttress. First Section is usually an ice pitch (steep). The gully above is straightforward with awkward slabby exit into large basin. Easiest exit from snow basin is up easy ridge on L or finish via 1, 2, or 3.

101 Overleaf left: Climbers at top of Gully 3, Ben Nevis. This Gully and Gully 4 are good descent routes to the CIC in good visibility

102 Overleaf right: The last pitch, Green Gully, Ben Nevis

103.5 **Raeburn's Buttress, Ordinary Route**
600ft grade IV+*: FA *H Raeburn, H MacRobert, D Arthur 1908*
This route goes up gully on S side, climbed for 200ft on easy
slabs. The gully divides here and encloses a further buttress.
Up R fork, for 100ft (narrowing) to a cave, ST chockstone, B.
R wall is ascended and further similar wall, leading to crack.
Reach crest of buttress on R, follow for 200ft to top. Last pitch
is steep edge going to level knife edge. (Can be avoided, TR R
into corner.)

Winter Hard Severe ($3\frac{1}{2}$–4 hours)*: FA *W D Brooker, J Taylor
January 1959*
Take approximately the summer line.

103 **Cousin's Buttress**
Grade IV*: FA (Summer) *C Walker, H Walker 1904*
Up same gully as for Raeburn's Buttress. At bifurcation go L
over easy slabs to top of buttress. The original route starts to L
well below bifurcation by grassy ledge halfway up buttress. The
rocks are steep to top of Buttress (IV). From pinnacle, the neck
joining buttress to peak is easily reached. From neck, route goes
L below smooth face past top of a gully and across awkward
corner to grass ledge. A few feet along ledge, avoiding easier
ground to L, up steep rocks for 200ft to platform almost level
with top of Raeburn's Buttress. Scrambling to steep rocks
forming summit wall of Carn Dearg (climbed slightly R of
actual summit).

103.SC **South Castle Gully**
700ft Winter, Very Difficult (1–2 hours)*: FA *W Brunskill,
W King, W Naismith April 1896*
This is normally an easy snow climb, though early in season one
pitch may give difficulty. Climb this by gangway on L wall.

103.NC **North Castle Gully**
700ft Winter, Moderate/Difficult (1–$1\frac{1}{2}$ hours)*: FA *J H Bell,
R Napier April 1896*
An easy gully, suitable for an easy day.

103 Carn Dearg, Castle Corrie climbs. The approach route is marked
round base of the Great Buttress. From the CIC Hut this is reached
via small gully which leads through the rocks just under Gully 5.
Make a rising traverse to foot of Great Buttress. 7 = Raeburn's
Buttress

103.CR **Castle Ridge**

1000ft grade II

This route is usually started just R of North Castle Gully, but can be started from lowest part of rocks in the Glen. Various lines and variations to top.

Winter Very Difficult (2–4 hours)*: FA *J N Collie, W W Naismith, G Thomson, M Travers April 1895*
This is the easiest of the big ridges. Start just below start of North Castle Gully, or lower down as illustrated. By the higher start the rocks of ridge crest just above the little gully offer the only unavoidable difficulty. Keep to the R above.

104.1 **Route 1**

700ft grade IV*: FA *A Hargreaves, G Graham Macphee, H Hughes 1931;* Variation Direct Start: FA *R L Plackett, W W Campbell 1941*
Start at lowest rocks of small buttress and ascend by R edge. Follow groove on R wall to join Route 1. Or, start to L of bottom rocks of small curved buttress, which is to lower L flank of buttress. Up to ledge and B; 45ft. Take R edge to big ledge; 60ft. Easy by grassy cracks to L to block B 30ft. above. TR L below groove to reach ST B at foot of slab; 20ft. Climb into groove and follow this to recess; 40ft B. Up R then L to ledge B; 40ft. Easy to top of minor buttress.

Walk to R to base of obvious chimney, up this finishing by grassy groove to recess and B; 70ft. Ascend R wall 20ft to B; 10ft. Regain the chimney above and climb to ST B; 50ft. Go L, ascend exposed slab to B at base of final chimney; 25ft. Up chimney to wide ledge; 40ft. Easy R and up easier rock to summit.

104 **Torro**

800ft grade VI+**: FA *J McLean, W Smith, W Gordon 1962*
Start 30ft L of Centurion at groove. Climb groove (one P), continue up to flake. Climb groove above to large flake. Up this on R-hand side, move back L and follow groove to good ST and flake B; 100ft. Continue up widening fault, cross bulge on L to gain edge of slab (P runner). TR L over slab, step round corner and up overhanging groove to good ST, B; 80ft. Diagonally R round bulge into crack, up this 20ft, go slightly R.

104 Carn Dearg Buttress from the CIC Hut. 2=start of Gully 5 and CR=Castle Ridge

and then up slab to good ST; 8oft. P B. Up slight crack, 25ft, step L on to higher slab (P runner). Up slab 8ft, climb overhang above trending L (one P), then groove above for 2oft to good ST; 7oft. P B. Up fault above 15ft, TR across slab on R to crack. Up crack to overhang, surmount this moving L-wards and follow a groove to grassy ST; 14oft. P B. Continue up fault to grassy ledge under large overhangs 1ooft P B. Go through overhangs using 7th pitch of Centurion. From B above this pitch TR L into steep corner. Use P to start and follow to grassy terrace.

104.3 Centurion

62oft grade —VI***: FA *D Whillans, R Downes 1956*

Start under prominent corner 1ooft L of Sassenach. Climb wall on L of corner to ledge, go R into groove and up to grass ledge; B; 5oft. Up steep corner above (good runners) ST on slab in overhung bay; 12oft. TR L to arete, easy up grooves and step R onto lip of large overhang and up to ST, P B; 8oft. Go back into corner, TR wall up to the L under overhanging crack, follow arete to ST; 7oft. Continue in same line up slabby grooves to small ST and block B; 7oft. Follow in same line, then L to ST, 6oft, before long TR pitch of Route 2 (not described). Climb up to overhang and TR L to slab, go L up to further overhang, step off detached flake and TR up L (delicate) onto big slab. Ascend this easily up to R to ST B under second tier of overhangs; 9oft. TR R, 2oft then direct up spiky arete to bulge. Step L above bulge into easy groove. Up to broad platform and easier ground.

104 The Bat

1oooft grade VI+**: FA *R Smith, D Haston 1959*

The obvious feature of route is high corner between Sassenach and Centurion. Go 5oft up first pitch of Centurion, then 15oft up corner until it steepens and TR top of slab on R. Up R round block, follow shelf to block B at top R end. 8oft stepdown and round to lower shelf; ascend corner on R. Climb short R wall to triangular slab. Enter overhanging corner on R and up to slab on R. TR R, round edge to B below Sassenach chimney. Climb overhanging corner 1oft L of Sassenach chimney, out onto slab on L. P B below great overhanging corner. Climb corner, three P used at and above halfway roof; 12oft. Continue up a fault bearing R; then up L end of ledge above chimney of Sassenach;

then up and L over bulge and continue to terrace; 100ft. Pitches 8, 9, 10, 11: TR L and climb up cracked bulge. Follow yellowish fault L-wards. Pass to R of overhangs and finish at top of Route 2.

104.4 Sassenach

800ft grade −VI*: FA *J Brown, D Whillans (through leads) 1954*
Below and R of prominent corner is a slab leaning against face. Climb sloping mossy ledges just L of this for 20ft to where it is possible to step R onto nose. TR L to base of crack. Up this to ST and B at top; 80ft. Follow up corner (using slings) to overhang. TR L and up grooves above, going L to ST and B; 60ft. Easy to bottom of corner; 30ft. Up chimney; 50ft. Up corner; 60ft. On up corner to grassy terrace; 60ft. On up terrace to base of V groove capped by overhang; 50ft. Up groove, 30ft until possible to step L onto ledge, follow up crack to base of further groove, ST and B; 110ft. Up groove by corner crack; 40ft. Go out R at top. In three further pitches climb groove to top.

105.T Titan's Wall

320ft grade V+ A2***: FA *I Clough, H MacInnes 1959*
This route is up great wall to R of Sassenach. Ascend (free climbing) first 50ft by cracks up centre of wall (a better alternative is to reach this point by climbing edge of buttress, 20ft then continuing up slab). Crack line is followed from overhang, trending R by artificial climbing to reach ledge. Go L along ledge until above overhang, ST and P B (120ft to here). 150ft back along ledge to crack line. Up bulges (artificial) and free climbing to ledge, B. 100ft up steep groove and L and along to grassy terrace. This is Sassenach. 48oft, pitches 7–12 of Sassenach.

105. The Shield Direct

220ft grade −VI*: FA *J R Marshall, G J Ritchie, R Marshall 1962*
Starts in corner just R of Titan's Wall. Climb corner, surmounting large roof at mid-height (three P) and in 4 pitches continue to join the Shield after its initial chimney pitch.

105 Overleaf left: Titan's Wall. This climb is situated between Waterfall Gully and Sassenach on the right side of Great Buttress

106 Overleaf right: Carn Dearg, Ben Nevis. Looking across to the Great Buttress from just below the CIC Hut

Bibliography

Avalanche Enigma Colin Fraser MURRAY
Mountaineering Alan Blackshaw PENGUIN HANDBOOK
Mountain Leadership Eric Langmuir SCPR & CCPR
Mountain Rescue & Cave Rescue Mountain Rescue Committee
Safety on Mountains CCPR

Index

220